MEXICO

WHAT EVERYONE NEEDS TO KNOW

MEXICO
WHAT EVERYONE NEEDS TO KNOW

RODERIC AI CAMP

OXFORD
UNIVERSITY PRESS

OXFORD

UNIVERSITY PRESS

Oxford University Press, Inc., publishes works that further
Oxford University's objective of excellence
in research, scholarship, and education.

Oxford   New York
Auckland   Cape Town   Dar es Salaam   Hong Kong   Karachi
Kuala Lumpur   Madrid   Melbourne   Mexico City   Nairobi
New Delhi   Shanghai   Taipei   Toronto

With offices in
Argentina   Austria   Brazil   Chile   Czech Republic   France   Greece
Guatemala   Hungary   Italy   Japan   Poland   Portugal   Singapore
South Korea   Switzerland   Thailand   Turkey   Ukraine   Vietnam

Copyright © 2011 by Oxford University Press, Inc.

Published by Oxford University Press, Inc.
198 Madison Avenue, New York, NY 10016

www.oup.com

Oxford is a registered trademark of Oxford University Press

Library of Congress Cataloging-in-Publication Data
Camp, Roderic A.
Mexico : what everyone needs to know / Roderic Ai Camp.
    p.   cm.
Includes bibliographical references and index.
ISBN 978-0-19-977387-9 (pbk.) — ISBN 978-0-19-977388-6 (cloth)
1. Mexico—Politics and government.   2. Mexico—Economic conditions.
3. Mexico—Economic policy.   4. National security—Mexico.
5. United States—Relations—Mexico.
6. Mexico—Relations—United States.   I. Title.
JL1281.C339 2011
972dc22   2011001655

1 3 5 7 9 8 6 4 2

Printed in the United States of America
on acid-free paper

To Ellie, Margot, and Ada, Who Want to Know Everything

CONTENTS

TABLES

ACKNOWLEDGMENTS

When Angela Chnapko, my editor at Oxford University Press, approached me about the new series What Everyone Needs to Know, I was struck by the press's imagination in attempting to reach a broader audience and hopefully educate Americans and other readers about multiple aspects of specific countries and their citizens. I owe my deep thanks to her in encouraging me to take on the challenge of writing this work in the midst of three other book projects. I always have pursued the broadest exploration of all aspects of things Mexican from art to intellectuals during my professional career, and it was a worthwhile and rewarding effort to reeducate myself in many of these areas. I also want to thank my wife, Emmy, for reinforcing Angela's enthusiasm for the project and for agreeing to my pursuit of two self-assigned questions a day in Claremont and Cooper Bay North in the beautiful spring and summer of 2010.

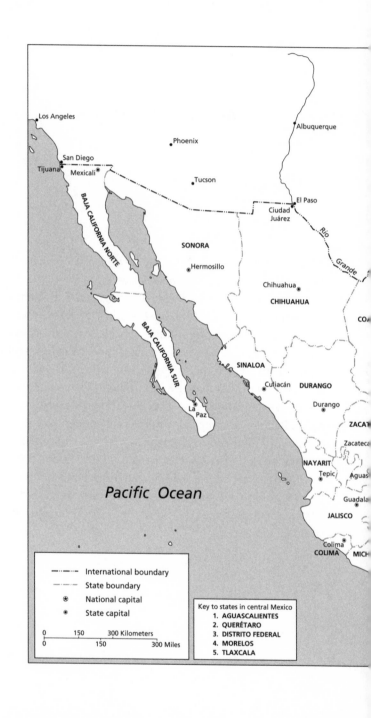

Los Angeles

Albuquerque

Phoenix

San Diego

Tijuana   Mexicali

Tucson

BAJA CALIFORNIA NORTE

El Paso

Ciudad
Juárez

Río

Grande

SONORA

Hermosillo

Chihuahua

CHIHUAHUA

COA

BAJA CALIFORNIA SUR

SINALOA

Culiacán   DURANGO

La
Paz

Durango

ZACAT

Zacateca

NAYARIT

Tepic   Aguas

Pacific Ocean

Guadala

JALISCO

Colima

COLIMA   MICH

International boundary

State boundary

⊛ National capital

⊙ State capital

0	150	300 Kilometers
0	150	300 Miles

Key to states in central Mexico
1. **AGUASCALIENTES**
2. **QUERÉTARO**
3. **DISTRITO FEDERAL**
4. **MORELOS**
5. **TLAXCALA**

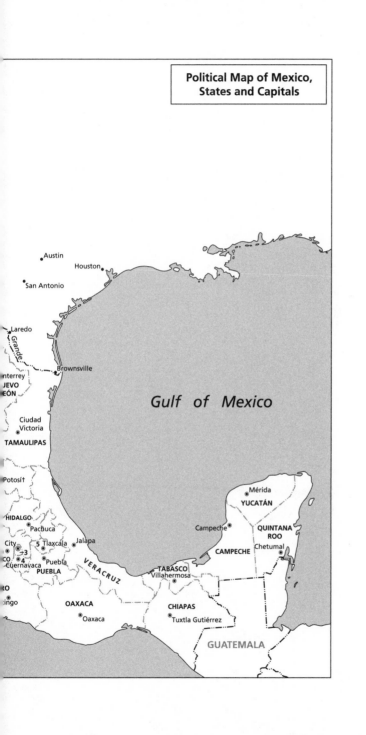

Political Map of Mexico, States and Capitals

Austin

Houston

San Antonio

Laredo

Grande

nterrey

Brownsville

JEVO
EÓN

Gulf of Mexico

Ciudad
Victoria

TAMAULIPAS

Potosít

Mérida

YUCATÁN

HIDALGO

Pachuca

Campeche

QUINTANA
ROO

City

5 Tlaxcala Jalapa

CO 3

Chetumal

CO 4

CAMPECHE

Cuernavaca Puebla

VERACRUZ

TABASCO

PUEBLA

Villahermosa

RO

ingo

OAXACA

CHIAPAS

Oaxaca

Tuxtla Gutiérrez

GUATEMALA

INTRODUCTION

Many scholarly friends from my generation who specialized
in Latin American studies or some other regional specialization have expressed an itch to accomplish two complementary professional, scholarly goals: write a novel set in
their country of specialization and perhaps even more challenging, a textbook. Writing the answers to some one hundred
questions about Mexico falls into a similar category. Any of us
who are interested in world affairs or the cultures of other
countries always have questions we want to ask about that
special place. Thus, it was a welcome invitation to write such
a book about Mexico, and I commend Oxford University
Press for initiating such a valuable series.

I am into my fifth decade of research on Mexico, having
begun my scholarly work in 1966 under the guidance of the
late historian Mario Rodríguez, a distinguished Central
Americanist. He would have approved of this project, which
brings together academic interests from a variety of disciplines. As suggested in the Table of Contents, I have begun
the book with a series of provocative questions raised
implicitly in most recent media accounts, or that have come
up repeatedly in my public speaking engagements among
general audiences and students. Some of these questions
address difficult political and security issues Mexico faces,
issues which naturally impact the United States. Because

Mexico and the United States share a nearly 2,000-mile border and a two-century contentious history that ended in Mexico losing half of its national territory to its northern neighbor, our relationship with Mexico, and the various influences ranging from cultural to economic emanating from one country to the other, also receive significant attention.

After touching on much of Mexico's historic political, social, economic, and cultural development during its colonial era, and the formative decades of the nineteenth century, the latter chapters focus on the impact of Mexico's decisive revolutionary decade of 1910–20, recognized through numerous bicentennial and centennial celebrations in both countries during 2010. To conclude, I answer numerous questions about how Mexico's democratic transition came about, a transition which lagged behind most other countries in the region. In the final section, I explore a number of questions focusing on where Mexico finds itself today as it undergoes changes in the process of democratic consolidation. It is my hope that in exploring the answers to many of the questions, the reader's interest will be sufficiently piqued to delve further into Mexico's fascinating culture and history, and its impact on the United States. A brief, highly selective bibliography in English follows the questions, including numerous Mexican authors, providing readers with a wide range of interpretations.

As has been the case of my preceding authors in the series, it is impossible to answer many of the questions without making references to some of the material that appears in the other answers. While I have tried to minimize such duplication throughout the individual answers, it is necessary to include certain interpretations and factual material more than once to completely and accurately answer distinctive questions.

PART I

MAJOR ISSUES FACING
MEXICO TODAY

1

SECURITY AND VIOLENCE IN MEXICO

Why does Mexico have so much drug violence today?

Mexico's drug problems emanate from the insatiable demand for drugs in the United States. Currently, the United States provides the largest market for drugs in the world. The level of demand for drugs by the United States rarely changes in spite of all the measures, successful and unsuccessful, that the government has tried to prevent drugs from entering the United States. In fact, drug experts suggest that the only likely decline in drug usage in the foreseeable future will be among cocaine users, not because of a successful strategy, but because a disproportionate percentage of cocaine users are baby boomers and their numbers are declining. The United States has spent most of its antidrug budget on an interdiction strategy, much of which has focused on the border with Mexico. As part of that strategy, it has encouraged the Mexican government for years to prevent the shipment of drugs from and through Mexico, and to destroy drug production in Mexico. To make that strategy more effective in Mexico, it urged the Mexican government to expand the role of the Mexican Army to carry out that task, given the ineffectiveness and corruption among civilian agencies both local and national.

When President Vicente Fox was elected in 2000, in spite of campaigning on a promise to withdraw the military from the drug war, he not only maintained their role, but also increased their presence. He improved the effectiveness of the military through increased cooperation with the attorney general, who in his first cabinet was himself a brigadier general. The improved coordination between civil and military authorities, as well as collaboration with the Drug Enforcement Agency and other U.S. officials, increased the number of drug leaders who were killed or captured. Those very successes, however, created a vacuum among the major drug cartels leading to intense, violent confrontations among the competing cartels for control over territory and new drug routes. By the end of the Fox administration, more than thirty thousand troops were engaged in this mission.

Felipe Calderón became president in 2006. He decided to confront the drug cartels more proactively by assigning roving battalions directly to those communities or regions where drug-related violence was most pronounced. In the first four years of his administration, he increased the numbers of troops and officers from both the army and navy to slightly more than fifty thousand, hoping to break up the large cartels into much smaller and more easily controlled units. This proactive strategy, while succeeding in capturing more top traffickers, not only has led to much higher levels of intra-cartel violence but also has increased the deaths of soldiers, police, prosecutors, and innocent bystanders, contributing to Mexico having a higher homicide rate in Latin America, most of it drug-related. It also has led to an increased level of human rights abuses by the armed forces. Increasing numbers of Mexicans, in response to the increasing levels of violence, now believe their personal security is compromised and that the government's strategy is largely responsible for that violence. Illustrative of the increased violence is the fact that from 2004 to the end of 2010, twenty-seven mayors have been murdered—fourteen of them in 2010 alone. In 2010, 15,273 individuals were murdered, compared with 9,614 executions in all of 2009, a 63 percent increase.

Has Mexico always had a drug problem?

Since Felipe Calderón became president in 2006, most of the news about Mexico published in the United States has focused on drug traffickers and drug-related violence that has been the consequence of the government's intense efforts to destroy the cartels. Whereas the level of drug-related violence and the high number of homicides are a recent phenomena, drug trafficking has been present in Mexico for decades. Mexico's long-term drug trafficking history is tied to the consumption of illegal products in the United States. When the United States prohibited the production and sale of alcohol in the 1920s and 1930s, Mexico and Canada both became sources of illegal shipments. Prohibition ended the illegal transportation of alcohol across the border, but the consumption of other illegal substances has grown, reflecting the huge population increase in the second half of the twentieth century. Mexico has been the source of drugs, such as marijuana, for decades and the source for the transshipments of drugs from South America. During the administration of Richard Nixon, the president declared a "War on Drugs," which focused U.S. resources on an interdiction strategy to prevent drugs from coming into the United States. During the administration of Miguel de la Madrid (1982–88), the United States encouraged Mexico to use the army to identify drug-producing farms and to destroy their crops. Battalions were sent from central Mexico to drug growing regions in the north, including states such as Sinaloa and Chihuahua, which currently are among the states most affected by drug cartels, typically spending six months of each year in pursuit of that task. In the following administration under Carlos Salinas de Gortari, the president attempted to expand the military's role in the drug interdiction strategy, going beyond destroying crops to capturing drug traffickers. The army made it known that it did not favor performing such a mission, and the president withdrew his request to expand its antidrug role. As large, organized cartels seized control over trafficking and production, the United States attempted to increase its collaboration with the Mexican government, and again to pressure the Mexican government to use their armed forces to achieve a more effective antidrug effort. Under President Ernesto Zedillo (1994–2000), the army accepted this expanded role in 1995, and the federal government began increasing the size of the army (it increased 25 percent from 1994–2009) and the amount of resources devoted to antidrug tasks. Expenditures for public security among all agencies increased 338 percent from 2000 through 2008. Furthermore, by the end of the Zedillo administration the consumption of drugs domestically increased significantly, creating a serious social problem. As the 2008 Addiction Survey in Mexico reported, the number of drug users in Mexico increased by a million between 2002 and 2008 (from 3.5 million to 4.5 million), and the number of Mexicans addicted to illegal drugs increased by 51 percent (to nearly half a million). Inhalable cocaine use almost doubled during the same period. Forty-three percent of those between the ages of 12 and 25 have been exposed to drug use, and half of those people have experimented with drugs, while 13 percent use drugs frequently.

Which areas of Mexico are most affected by drug violence, who are the primary targets, and does the violence spill across the border?

One of the most important misconceptions about drug-related violence in Mexico is that all locales are equally affected. In 2010, the Mexican government provided its first comprehensive analysis of drug-related violence based on previously classified official statistics. The officially documented murders at that time, 22,700 (August 2010), revealed that 80 percent of the murders since Calderón took office (December 1, 2006) occurred in just 6 percent of Mexico's 2,456 municipalities. The report also concluded that as of that date, seven violent major regional conflicts among the leading drug cartels were taking place, and that 8,236 homicides (36 percent) could be attributed to just the conflict between the Sinaloa Cartel, concentrated in northwest Mexico along the Gulf of Cortez, and the Juárez Cartel, which is located across the border from El Paso, Texas, in Ciudad Juárez. This conflict explains why Ciudad Juárez has been ranked as one of the most dangerous cities in the world. These two cartels are battling for control of overland routes for illegal drugs across the Texas border. Further, the Sinaloa Cartel is also confronting other major cartels, including the Beltrán Leyva organization, the Gulf and Zetas organization, and the Arellano Félix organization, which combined account for 48 percent of the remaining drug-related homicides. There are also conflicts between the Gulf and Zeta organizations, as well as the Michoacán-based Familia and Beltrán Leyva organizations. On a state-by-state basis since December 2006, Chihuahua accounts for the highest level of murders at 30 percent of the total, followed by Sinaloa (13 percent), Baja California (6.3 percent), Michoacán (5.4 percent), Tamaulipas (3 percent), and Nuevo León (2.6 percent). Three of these states, Baja California, Chihuahua, and Tamaulipas, border the United States, and a fourth, Nuevo León, shares a 9-mile border with Texas. Surprisingly, given the concentration of drug-related homicides along the border on the Mexican side, an equal level of violence has not occurred on the northern side. One of the most interesting contrasts reinforcing this finding is the level of homicides between El Paso, Texas, and Ciudad Juárez, Chihuahua, since El Paso boasts one of the lowest homicide rates for a metropolitan area in the United States. However, drug cartel violence has spilled over in other ways, linked strongly to Mexican drug trafficking connections throughout the United States and Canada. Murders, kidnappings, assaults, and home invasions have occurred in such diverse places as Vancouver, British Columbia; Phoenix and Tucson, Arizona; Birmingham, Alabama; Billings, Montana; and Boston. The

Drug Enforcement Agency identified drug distribution networks linked to the Mexican cartels in 230 cities in 2009, up significantly from 2006.

As these figures indicate, the leading cause of drug-related deaths is homicides perpetrated by drug cartels against each other. The vast majority of victims are employed by the cartels. Indeed, the government claims that 90 percent of the victims are affiliated with the cartels. Nevertheless, public officials, police, members of the armed forces, journalists, and innocent bystanders have been murdered by drug traffickers. Some of these victims have been in the employ of one cartel while working against the interests of another cartel. Most, however, have been killed because they were opposed to or investigating drug cartels and cartel ties to public officials. Such killings, some of them high profile, have expanded the impact of drug-related violence to the larger public. For example, twenty-seven mayors have been assassinated since 2004. Of those officials, fourteen were killed in 2010. Based on statistics compiled by the Trans-Border Institute of the University of San Diego and the *Reforma* newspaper, during the last decade, drug-related homicides in Mexico have increased dramatically since President Calderón took office, but especially since 2008. During the first four years of the Fox administration (2001–04), the number of drug-related homicides remained fairly stable, ranging from 1,080 to 1,304 yearly. As Fox increased efforts to control drug cartel criminal activity, those figures increased to 1,776 in 2005 and 2,120 in 2006. In 2008, the figures increased dramatically to 6,837, then to 9,614 in 2009, and by the end of 2010, it had reached an extraordinary 15,273. Drug-related murders, as a percentage of the total homicide rate in Mexico, also have increased significantly. The homicide rate in Mexico was following a fairly consistent decline from the 1950s until 2007, which witnessed the lowest homicide rate of that decade. In 2007, 26 percent of all homicides were attributable to drug-related violence, rising to 37 percent in 2008 and 43 percent in 2009.

How are Mexico's security problems America's problems?

The most important security problem in Mexico today is the significant presence of drug cartels and the extent of their influence in Mexico and the rest of North America. Contemporary drug cartels in Mexico are a broader reflection of organized crime. These cartels have expanded into dozens of other activities, ranging from bribery, kidnapping, and extortion to laundering money in legal business, such as major Mexican soccer teams. Given the nature of their business, to produce drugs in and to transport drugs through and from Mexico to the United States, the largest market for illegal substances in the world, drug cartels have increased their competition for control of the border, including illegal trafficking, as a defensive strategy against the Mexican government's aggressive posture since Calderón took office in 2006. One of the concerns of Homeland Security in the United States is that terrorist groups will use these routes, many of which are now controlled by drug trafficking organizations, including the Zetas—one of the eight leading drug trafficking organizations (DTOs)—to cross surreptitiously into the United States. According to the U.S. government, criminal organizations generally are increasing their ties to terrorist organizations. In Mexico, the only known ties between drug cartels and a designated terrorist organization is to the Revolutionary Armed Forces of Colombia (FARC) and the United Self Defense of Colombia (AUC), both of which have been tied to drug traffickers in Colombia.

Because Mexican drug cartels have to market most of their drugs in the United States, they have developed numerous linkages to criminal elements north of the border. One of their strongest links is to juvenile gangs operating in most metropolitan areas. They also are associated with gangs in major Mexican border cities, for example Ciudad Juárez, across from El Paso, Texas. Therefore, a recognized concern on the part of law enforcement agencies in the United States is the extent to which drug cartels are financing and directing the activities of juvenile gangs in this country.

Drug cartels also are compromising dozens of government officials in the United States. Individuals working for the United States government, including in the American embassy in Mexico City, as well as the former director of the Nogales sector of the Immigration and Naturalization Service, have been in the pay of the cartels. The cartels also support significant criminal activities in the United States beyond the illegal sale of drugs, notably money laundering and the purchase and importation of illegal weapons from the United States, largely from gun shops and shows in Texas. Billions of dollars in drug profits are shipped back on trailer trucks across the border into Mexico.

The presence of criminal activities extends to the serious threat against the sovereignty of Mexican governmental institutions on the local, state, and national levels. Drug profits are so extensive in Mexico, an estimated $25 billion to $40 billion a year, that cartels are bribing governmental officials at all levels, including mayors, governors, and top federal law enforcement officials. They also are involving themselves directly in financing electoral campaigns to such an extent that the incumbent party, the National Action Party (PAN), chose its gubernatorial candidate in 2010 for the border state of Tamaulipas from central party headquarters in order to prevent any undue influence by potentially compromised local politicians. During this same campaign, a drug cartel murdered the Institutional Revolutionary Party's candidate shortly before the election. The ability of the political leadership in Mexico at all levels, and therefore the sovereignty of governmental institutions, is at stake if these institutions cannot protect the general citizenry and reduce the high levels of perceived insecurity affecting nearly two-thirds of the population in 2010. Such levels of insecurity related to levels of crime, real and perceived, also affect the degree of support Mexicans would give to democratic governance. Therefore, the political model itself is under duress.

What is the origin of the drug cartels and which organizations are the major cartels?

The growing of illegal drugs has a long history in Mexico, especially marijuana and opium poppies. The production of both of these drugs increased significantly during World War II when the U.S. government asked Mexico to increase marijuana production for the hemp and poppy production for morphine when Asian routes for these products were blocked by the Axis powers. After the war, many of the growers continued to produce these crops for the illegal drug market. In the 1970s and 1980s, the Mexican army, at the request of the president, sent battalions to Sinaloa, Durango, and Chihuahua to destroy drug-producing fields. These three states today, along with Guerrero in the south, account for nearly 60 percent of the drug-related violence in Mexico. The United States, in response to drugs coming from South America through the Caribbean, closed down the air and sea routes, which redirected drug transshipments overland through Mexico. The existing drug trafficking organization in the late 1980s, led by Miguel Ángel Félix Gallardo, was responsible for developing the antecedents to many of the current cartels in Mexico, assigning different territories to individual families. These families increased their domestic production of drugs rather than merely serving as transshipment agents for the Colombian cartels. Many of the Mexican DTOs today are led by individuals who represent the third generation of traffickers organic to Mexico. Currently, eight major drug trafficking organizations are operating in Mexico. They are the Beltrán Leyva Cartel, which established an alliance with Los Zetas, formerly a group employed by the Gulf Cartel, but they have gone out on their own, emulating leading cartels. Another cartel, La Familia, concentrated in the state of Michoacán along the west coast of central Mexico, is involved in extortion and kidnapping, and has formed an alliance with the Gulf Cartel against the Beltrán Leyva organization and

Los Zetas. The Gulf Cartel, based in Matamoros, Tamaulipas, along the Texas border in the northeast corner, remains one of the leading cartels in Mexico. The Juárez Cartel in Chihuahua, which has declined in influence, has been conducting an all-out war against the Sinaloa Cartel for control of drug routes through central and northwestern Mexico. The Sinaloa Cartel, often referred to as the Pacific drug trafficking organization, is also fighting against the Gulf Cartel for control of its territory. The Tijuana Cartel, which also controlled routes along the Pacific Northwest, has been weakened by the loss of some of its top leadership. Finally, Los Negros, similar to Los Zetas, originally enforcers for the Gulf Cartel, was an enforcement arm of the Sinaloa Cartel, but has become an independent organization. These drug-trafficking organization alliances are fluid and change frequently as the Mexican government attempts to break them up into smaller, less powerful organizations. They often use corrupt officials to lessen the influence of their opponents while protecting themselves from security forces.

What role has Mexico played in the U.S. Northern Command?

When the United States was attacked by terrorists on September 11, 2001, one of the structural changes which came about as a result of the government's response to those events was the creation of U.S. Northern Command. This is a coordinated defense organization, located at Peterson Air Force Base in Colorado Springs, incorporating the collaboration of Canada and Mexico. The rationale for such a structure in response to the global threat of terrorism was that the United States could not effectively protect its borders, and therefore its domestic security, without the assistance of its two neighbors. Despite the creation of Northern Command, Mexico refused to participate directly in the unified decision-making structure and would not send a permanent liaison officer to reside at Northern Command. Mexico's Secretariat of National Defense was willing to cooperate with the United

States on certain security matters, but did not want to become involved directly or formally in a joint, security structure.

The U.S. military repeatedly has asked Mexico to actively join this command structure. As the United States and Mexico began to increase their collaboration in battling the drug cartels in Mexico, Mexico's level of trust toward the American military increased, especially after 2006. In Mexico, the naval ministry took the first step in cementing stronger relations with its counterpart in the United States. The navy was the first service to join the United States and other countries in joint naval exercises, suggesting that they have a more open attitude toward other countries' militaries, including those of the United States. For example, the Mexican Navy participated in the UNITAS Gold exercises in April–May 2009. Naval officers historically have been more likely than their counterparts in the army to have received advance training in the United States. In 2007, they assigned a commander to the Northern Command staff.

Northern Command, in an attempt to broaden its relationship with other defense and security-related decision-makers in Mexico, also extended invitations to members of congress, and to government officials with security-related responsibilities. Not to be outdone by the navy, the Mexican Army finally decided to assign its own liaison in 2009. This is the first time the Mexican Army has designated a specific officer to represent its interests in a U.S. military structure. This decision represents a significant change in attitude on the part of the Mexican military leadership. All American and Mexican military services have increased their collaboration with the implementation of the Mérida Initiative, a U.S. congressional program designed to increase U.S. financial assistance and war materiel in Mexico's war on drugs.

What do Mexicans consider to be the most important issues facing the country?

Mexicans are similar to the majority of citizens from other countries in caring most about economic and social issues that affect the quality of their daily lives. When specific countries are not facing unique issues, citizens are concerned about the economy and the rate of economic growth. For many decades, beginning in the 1970s, ordinary citizens and Mexican leadership both have been concerned with and focused on the country's slow rate of growth. Despite some individual years when growth rates have been strong, Mexico's economy has not been able to keep up with the numbers of Mexicans who are eligible to join the workforce each year. In each of the last three presidential races—1994, 2000, and 2006—regardless of whether the economy has been performing well or not, economic issues generally have been most important. In fact, on average, the typical Mexican since 2001 has viewed the country's economic situation as worse than the previous year (see Table 1). During this past decade, generally 60 percent or more have viewed the economy in a negative light. In 2009 and 2010, approximately 80 percent considered the economic situation to be worse than the previous year versus only 12 percent who saw it as better.

When Mexicans are asked what they perceive to be the most important problem their country faces, they typically rank "economic crisis" in first place. This was true in eight out of the last ten years. (In 2005 and 2006, they considered insecurity to be more important than the economic situation.) Other issues that top the list of those that are most important include unemployment, poverty, corruption, low salaries, taxes, and inflation. However, if one combines all the economically related responses, nearly half or more of all Mexicans choose an economic issue as the most important. In 2009 and 2010, approximately a third of Mexicans ranked the economic crisis first, followed by nearly a fifth of Mexicans who placed insecurity in first place and an additional 17 percent who viewed unemployment as most significant. If we lump together the leading issues related to insecurity, drug trafficking, and corruption, nearly a third of Mexicans in 2010 considered these issues most important.

Table 1 What do Mexicans consider to be their country's most important problem?

Issue	Year									
	2001	2002	2003	2004	2005	2006	2007	2008	2009	2010
Economic Crisis	23	28	25	23	18	17	24	28	38	32
Insecurity	20	19	18	17	25	25	22	20	17	20
Unemployment	15	15	18	22	19	21	15	14	16	17
Poverty	12	14	14	13	12	13	11	10	8	8
Drug Trafficking	2	1	2	1	2	2	6	7	5	6
Corruption	5	7	7	10	10	7	6	6	4	5
Low Salaries	2	3	2	2	3	3	3	4	3	3
Inflation	3	1	1	1	1	1	2	3	3	2
Taxes	...	...	...	...	...	1	1	1	2	2

Source: Adapted from www.consulta.com.mx, "Economía, gobierno y política," April 2010.

Does Mexico exercise political sovereignty throughout the republic?

In November 2008, the U.S. Joint Forces Command of the Department of Defense issued an official report entitled *Joint Operating Environment, Challenges and Implications for the Future Joint Force*. In a section on weak and failing states, it suggested that "in terms of worst-case scenarios for the Joint Force, two large and important states bear consideration for a rapid and sudden collapse: Pakistan and Mexico." It went on to conclude that, "the Mexican possibility may seem less likely, but the government, its politicians, police, and judicial infrastructure are all under sustained assault and pressure by criminal gangs and drug cartels. How that internal conflict turns out over the next several years will have a major impact on the stability of the Mexican state. Any descent by Mexico into chaos would demand an American response based on the serious implications for homeland security alone."

As can be imagined, this provocative statement, without any additional evidence, caused widespread reaction in Mexico. Mexico was not nor is it bordering on being a failed state. Nevertheless, three years after this statement was issued, to what extent does Mexico exercise control over its national territory and governance structures? (See the question on Mexico's security in this chapter.) The level of control is indeed a significant measure of the stability and strength of a sovereign state. The degree to which drug cartels continue to infringe on the sovereignty of the civil governance structure in Mexico remains largely unchanged. On the local level, in various rural municipalities, drug cartels have threatened municipal leaders and police to such an extent that they are no longer functioning independently, or they have abandoned their positions altogether. The conditions of such municipalities change over time, thus the lack of political sovereignty is not necessarily continuous.

Moreover, if we go beyond overt control by criminal organizations and include their indirect control over political leaders and police forces, the compromising effects on political sovereignty is far more extensive, and in many cases unknown. Numerous mayors have been arrested for being in the pay of the drug cartels. Most police departments in Mexico are compromised by drug cartel bribery and threats. Given the level of corruption in the police, specifically drug-related corruption, it is impossible to protect potential witnesses who would testify against drug traffickers and their associates. Given the judicial reforms under way, in which judges are now demanding more comprehensive evidence of criminal guilt, witnesses, just as they would in the U.S. justice system, play a critical role in the successful prosecution and conviction of criminals. Because drug cartels are pursuing other forms of criminal activity, including the intimidation and bribery of local businesses, these activities also raise the question of how much control local authorities actually exercise in their communities.

2

MEXICO'S ECONOMIC DEVELOPMENT

How poor is Mexico?

The most serious problem in Mexico today is poverty. Indeed, as General Clemente Vega, President Fox's secretary of National Defense once suggested, it is the number one national security problem in Mexico. There is no question that several of Mexico's other leading social and political issues are strongly linked to the extent and depth of poverty in Mexico. They include drug production and trafficking, political corruption, human rights abuses, and lack of political participation. Economists traditionally measure poverty on the basis of income per capita. The United Nations has set a world standard by which countries can be compared. That standard measure of poverty is an individual who earns less than $2 per day. The UN has generated a second, more severe category, "absolute poverty," which is also defined by income. In this case the definition is $1 per person daily.

According to those figures, when Mexico achieved electoral democracy in 2000, approximately 50 percent of the population qualified as falling into the poverty category, and half of those into the absolute category. The federal government under President Zedillo (1994–2000) began seriously addressing the level of poverty, and by the end of Vicente Fox's administration in 2006, figures estimated that Mexico was able to reduce poverty levels to as low as 43 percent. Unfortunately, poverty figures have risen again after 2008 due to the severe recession. As analyst Miguel Székely has noted, a more sophisticated way of defining poverty is to evaluate it by three criteria: food, capabilities, and assets. Food poverty is measured by an adequate monthly per capita income necessary to purchase a basic basket of food. By that standard, more than 60 percent of Mexicans were poor in the 1950s, compared with only 14 percent in 2006. Capabilities poverty is the minimum amount of money necessary to achieve acceptable levels of health and education while meeting the food poverty test. More than 70 percent of Mexicans failed that test in the 1950s compared with 21 percent toward the end of the Fox presidency. Finally, asset poverty describes an individual who can meet the previous two standards but does not earn enough for minimum levels of shelter, clothing, and transportation, a condition which described nearly 90 percent of Mexicans sixty years ago, but affected 53 percent of the population in 2006. It took Mexico thirteen years, from 1994 to 2007, after a severe economic crisis in the late 1990s, to raise household income back to 1994 levels. Some estimates suggest that Mexico's economically marginal population will have risen to 48 percent when the 2010 census is completed and analyzed.

How is Mexico addressing its poverty?

An examination of poverty in Mexico over many years demonstrates that Mexico has been able to reduce poverty levels significantly since the mid-twentieth century. Those same figures, however, suggest how uneven those efforts have been. During the years of Mexico's so called "Economic Miracle," which marked a period of stable economic growth from the late 1950s to the early 1970s, poverty levels declined across all areas of measurement. In the early 1950s the number of Mexicans with inadequate income to purchase basic foodstuffs was 62 percent, the percentage unable to provide for education and health care was 73, and the percentage without adequate housing was 88. By 1982, at the beginning of the Miguel de la Madrid administration, those figures had declined to 22 percent, 30 percent, and 53 percent, respectively. Those figures essentially remained stagnant for the next twelve years, showing no change until the beginning of the Ernesto Zedillo administration (1994–2000). Under Zedillo, and with the advent of the North American Free Trade Agreement, these poverty measurements increased significantly, generally by 15 percent or more during the first years of his administration. By 1996, greater numbers of Mexicans began to leave each of these three poverty categories. By 2005 the figures declined to slightly below 1982 levels.

The recent declines can largely be attributed to Mexican programs designed specifically to alleviate poverty. Social expenditures by the federal government increased nearly 75 percent between 1996 and 2008. More important, the two major antipoverty programs of the Mexican government during those years, *Progresa* and *Oportunidades*, increased dramatically, not only in real terms, from 466 million pesos in 1997 to 38.2 billion pesos in 2008, but also as a percentage of the social budget. For example, expenditures for Oportunidades, which is a program that pays families a monthly sum for each child attending school, went from two-tenths of a percent of the social budget in 1997 to 3.4 percent in 2008, a seventeen-fold increase. During the first two years of the Calderón administration, this program alone accounted for a fifth of the government's antipoverty expenditures.

The Mexican government has devoted resources to Oportunidades because analysts from the World Bank and the Inter-American Development Bank believe that increasing the level of education is a crucial variable in eliminating long-term poverty rates. Despite these efforts, the increases and decreases in the level of poverty in the last three decades clearly suggest that periodic economic crises, often tied to the health of the U.S. economy, significantly alter the distribution of income in Mexico. During most of these periods, little change has taken place in the distribution of income. From 1989 to 2000, the bottom 10 percent of the population earned one and one half percent of the national income, while the top 10 percent of the population accounted for 40 percent of national income. From 2000 to 2006, for the first time in more than a decade, the percentage of national income assigned to the top income decile decreased significantly, from 40.3 to 34.5 percent, while the lowest group increased their share from 1.5 to 2.4 percent. Despite the proven success of the antipoverty programs, critics have argued for years that Mexico has done little to increase the efficiency of tax collections, thus limiting their ability to redistribute income through governmental programs.

What is the economic relationship between Mexico and the United States?

Mexico and the United States have shared a significant economic relationship for nearly two centuries. The two most important traditional components of that relationship have been trade and direct foreign investment by Americans in Mexico. The differences in the size of the two economies and the per capita income of the workforce have determined numerous aspects of the relationship. Economists describe this relationship as asymmetrical. Even though Mexico is our second largest trading partner, and the United States is its most important trading partner, the economic impact of the United States on Mexico is far more important than that of Mexico on the United States. Any significant downturn in the United States economy typically produces an adverse effect on Mexico's economy, including its exports to its northern neighbor. Eighty percent of Mexican exports in 2009 went to the United States. The severe recession of 2008, producing massive global consequences, has been far more significant for Mexico than for other Latin American trading partners.

The historic economic relationship between the two countries, as measured by direct foreign investment by the United States, led Mexico to create a series of restrictions on foreign control over the economy after 1920. Those restrictions, for many decades, limited investment in Mexico because all foreigners, including Americans, were not permitted to have a controlling interest in Mexican or jointly owned firms. When President Carlos Salinas (1988–94) decided to pursue a trading block strategy for accelerating Mexican economic growth, he initially approached the European Union, not wanting to increase Mexico's dependence on the United States. In addition to negotiating a commercial treaty with the United States and Canada, the North American Free Trade Agreement (NAFTA), Salinas removed many of the restrictions on foreigners, resulting in greater investment from the United States and other countries. In 2009, Mexico received $11.6 billion in direct foreign investment (down 51 percent from 2008, due to the recession), half of which came solely from the United States.

The asymmetrical relationship between the size and income levels of the two economies has led to a huge influx of immigrants from Mexico to the United States in search of jobs. Those immigrants, both legal and illegal, sent back $26 billion in 2007 (averaging $21 billion in recent years) to family members in Mexico, contributing significantly to economic growth, especially in smaller communities and rural areas. Again, as a consequence of the recession, those remittance figures declined 3.6 percent in 2008, for the first time since the government has kept records, and declined an additional 13 percent in 2009, for an estimated total of only $22 billion. According to the Mexican government, remittances from relatives abroad represents close to 19 percent of total income for urban Mexican households and 27 percent for rural households.

What is the impact of NAFTA on Mexico?

President Carlos Salinas, a trained economist, believed that a positive economic future for Mexico required the country to become part of an economic bloc, making it more competitive in world markets. Given the country's historical and disproportionate reliance on the United States for imports and exports, the president sought to link Mexico to the European Union. Europe, facing the additional weak economies from the recently devolved Eastern European states, demurred. Instead, Salinas and President George Bush collaborated on developing a North American Free Trade Agreement with Canada, after years of negotiation. The treaty went into effect on January 1, 1994, the precise day of the Zapatista National Liberation Army (Zapatistas) uprising against the government in Chiapas. This uprising symbolized the resistance of indigenous peasants to the treaty.

NAFTA has produced many different types of influence on Mexico, ranging from environmental consequences to labor rights. During the negotiating process, in anticipation of congressional approval in favor of the treaty, Mexican leadership responded to pressures to make elections more plural and transparent. Indirectly, the Mexican government's overwhelming desire to achieve such a trade agreement moved Mexico more rapidly along the path of democratic political development. NAFTA negotiations also led to greater public awareness about international cooperation economically and potentially politically. Surprising to many Mexican analysts was the fact that a majority of Mexicans, even before the approval of the treaty, viewed such an agreement, if it would improve their economic situation, in a positive light. Ten years after the implementation of NAFTA, the Chicago Council on Foreign Relations did a survey, finding that 78 percent of Mexicans thought NAFTA was good for the U.S. economy compared to 44 percent who viewed it as positive for Mexico. Fifty percent of Mexicans considered it good for Mexican business, and nearly half assessed it as positive for creating jobs in Mexico. Two-fifths of Mexicans believed it had improved their standard of living compared with 35 percent who considered it as negatively affecting it. Mexicans were evenly divided on its impact on the environment.

Recent analysts agree that NAFTA dramatically increased the volume and value of trade between the two countries. Moreover, economists attribute increased investment from the United States in the manufacturing sector to NAFTA. The agreement also has altered Mexico's own labor standards and made them correspond more closely to international standards. During the first decade of this century, exports accounted for one third of its economy and half the jobs created since 1995. Yet, despite these consequences, Mexico's overall economic growth since NAFTA has not been promising, nor has the agreement had a positive effect on income distribution. A recent Carnegie Foundation analysis of studies on NAFTA concluded, "It seems clear that NAFTA's promise of broad-based dynamic growth did not come true in Mexico."

What is the state of Mexico's economy today?

Mexico is the twelfth largest economy in the world in gross domestic product, but ranked only 60th in GDP per capita in 2009. In contrast, Spain is the ninth largest economy based on GDP but ranks 26th in GDP per capita. From 1980 to 2000, Mexico's GDP per capita grew only 15 percent compared with 98 percent for Chile. In terms of global competitiveness, the World Economic Forum Global Competitiveness Index has typically ranked Mexico in the bottom half of all countries since 2001. It has not improved on this rank, placing 60th out of 133 countries in 2009. Finally, Transparency International ranks countries on perception of corruption, based on market and governance conditions. Since 1999, Mexico's position in that rank has declined from fifty-eight out of ninety-nine countries surveyed to eighty-nine out of 180.

By 2005, Mexico had achieved a stable currency and close to a balanced budget. Yet, it faces numerous economic challenges, reflected in some of these rankings. The most important challenges it confronts presently are how to address the level of poverty that exists in the country and how to reduce the level of inequality in income, a reflection of that poverty. The most difficult challenge to its economy in the future is a dramatically shifting demographic distribution in the population. Currently, there are nine children younger than twenty for every adult age sixty-five and older. By 2050, the United Nations projects that the number of adults older than sixty-five (20 percent of the population) will be equal to the number of Mexican children, a ratio comparable to that of the United States. Mexico must address now how to support that elderly population in the future, when those in the work force will account for a much smaller percentage of Mexicans. It will not have the economic resources to support such a population once those ratios are altered.

Why has Mexico not been able to achieve a closer relationship between the GDP of the economy and that of per capita GDP? Economists have provided numerous explanations for the Mexican case. Various studies have recommended increasing the educational levels of its population. In the last decade, for example, more than 40 percent of the citizens aged twenty-five to sixty-four in Chile and Argentina obtained upper secondary education (87 percent in the United States), but only 13 percent of Mexicans achieved an equivalent education. In fact, more than a quarter of this same population had not graduated from the sixth grade, an essential component of improving human capital. Mexico needs to improve education levels to stay competitive with China and India, both of which have taken numerous jobs away from Mexico in the global market. Mexico also must reform its excessive labor market regulations, which discourage new businesses and increase the costs of doing business, suggesting why the World Bank ranked Mexico in 129th place out of 133 countries on the flexibility of its labor market. Mexico also remains highly uncompetitive in numerous sectors of the economy. For example, Telmex controls 85 percent of landline phones, while two companies, Televisa and TV Azteca, account for 95 percent of television programs. Other similarly controlled sectors include cement and bread. The number of companies on the stock market is also highly concentrated. Extended families continue to control major shares of leading companies. It is difficult to raise venture capital in Mexico and to compete in monopolized sectors. Finally, Mexico ranked at the bottom, with Guatemala, for non-oil tax revenues when Calderón took office, making tax reform a top priority.

What kind of economic model does Mexico follow?

When Mexico created the Constitution of 1917, a reading of the provisions suggested that it would pursue a modified, capitalist model, in which the state was assigned a larger role in the economic lives of its citizens. Its most direct intervention into the economy ascribed subsoil resources, including petroleum and minerals, as belonging to all Mexicans, and therefore to be managed by the state. This constitutional provision ultimately led to direct government control over the oil industry after 1938, a decision which has hampered Mexico's economic expansion in the last two decades. The government has relied excessively on those resources to fund federal programs and has unwisely spent rather than saved those resources for lean years when other sources of revenue declined. The Constitution of 1917 was also revolutionary in terms of designing provisions to achieve a higher level of social justice and equality. The document included a provision providing for a social security program long before it was considered by the United States. Unfortunately, Mexico was unable to implement that program until 1943.

Mexico's private sector for the remainder of the twentieth century often found itself at odds with the government, a feature of many capitalist models. But a component of the Institutional Revolutionary Party's rhetoric for much of this period, at least in public, was to exclude the business community as part of political support while carving out agrarian and labor sectors composed of government-controlled unions, as two of the cornerstones of the incumbent party. In the 1970s the federal government increased its control over numerous private sector enterprises, including restaurants and hotels, extending well beyond the traditional subsoil sectors. State control, direct and indirect, reached a high point with the nationalization of the banking and insurance industries in 1982, under President José López Portillo. It has been estimated that indirectly, by controlling the mortgages of numerous enterprises through the banks, that the government, in effect, controlled approximately 85 percent of the economy.

Mexico's economic history since 1982 has been marked by neo-liberal economic reforms that returned the financial institutions back to private hands, decreased restrictions on foreign investment, increased trade dramatically since 1995, and reduced state control over labor and other social actors since 2000. Despite these and other significant changes promoting the growth and size of the private sector, certain notable features continue to characterize Mexico's capitalist economic model. Citizen views of state versus private sector control of the economy continue to be heavily influenced by the constitutional and experiential heritage of the twentieth century. For example, in a survey completed by the Parametría polling firm in 2007, nearly three-quarters of Mexicans agreed with the statement that the government should control the economy. Only one-fifth thought the economy should be in the hands of the private sector. When asked if the private sector should increase its participation in the electric and the petroleum industries, a major reform advocated by the Calderón administration, 56 percent and

55 percent respectively said no. By contrast, only a fourth of the population favored the change.

An equally important feature of the private sector that extends back well before the twentieth century is the degree of control exercised by a small number of capitalist families over the economy. Of the largest one hundred companies in Mexico in 2001, forty-nine were controlled by foreigners or by the government. Of the remaining fifty-one firms, thirteen were not even listed on the stock exchange. Ninety-two percent of all sales revenues corresponded to the top 100 companies, with the top fifty companies accounting for 79 percent. An analysis of thirty-four of the fifty-one domestically owned companies where adequate information was available revealed that family members controlled an absolute majority or more of the shares, in many cases as high as 60 to 90 percent of shares. Moreover, twenty-five of the companies' presidents or chief executive officers were family members, demonstrating an extraordinary continuity and control by leading entrepreneurial families.

What does the Mexican economic model teach us about development?

During the 1950s and 1960s, when Mexico produced a long period of consistent economic growth known as the "Mexican Miracle," it relied heavily on a strategy of industrialization and urban expansion. Its industrialization strategy was based heavily on a popular economic theory from that era known as "import substitution industrialization," commonly referred to as the ISI strategy and popularized by economists associated with the Economic Commission for Latin America (CEMLA), a regional organization affiliated with the United Nations. The basic premise of this strategy was that developing countries should attempt to decrease their dependency on the developed economies by expanding and diversifying their own economies through industrialization. To protect their incipient national industries against the well-established producers of similar products from the developed economies, they needed to impose tariff barriers against imports of those same products.

By the 1970s, this strategy was no longer producing high levels of economic growth. Furthermore, numerous academic studies of this economic period revealed that in spite of the year-to-year growth, the real income of most working-class Mexicans did not improve significantly. Furthermore, many Mexican industries were not competitive with their counterparts in other economies. It has been argued that a major explanation for the lack of industrial competitiveness is that the tariff barriers should have been reduced incrementally over time and should not have remained permanently in effect.

In 1982, a new generation of Mexican political leaders, many of whom were trained at graduate programs in leading economics departments in the United States, exercised control over the top federal agencies that determined government macroeconomic policy. This new generation of leaders, typically referred to as technocrats, offered a new strategy based on global competition, believing that by associating Mexico with a powerful trading bloc in the United States and Canada and reductions on import tariffs on goods coming from the two countries, it could improve the size, quality, and competitiveness of Mexican firms. This new strategy, again based on trade patterns, did increase Mexican economic growth, but as recent studies of the North American Free Trade Agreement have shown, it has had little impact on the distribution of wealth and the reduction of income inequality. (See question on NAFTA in this chapter.) The Mexican models for the last half-century, in order to reduce poverty and income inequality, require government policies that focus specifically on anti-poverty strategies. The economy alone, regardless of the rate of growth, has not been able to overcome ingrained structural problems. Higher investments in elementary and secondary education, in antipoverty programs, and the adaptation of a progressive and more comprehensive tax structure, are necessary complementary policies to achieve the benefits of growth for all Mexicans.

Why is Mexico City so polluted and can these conditions be altered?

For decades, Mexico City earned a reputation as one of the most polluted metropolitan areas in the world. In fact, in 1992, it was ranked the most polluted metropolis in the world by the United Nations, and the most dangerous for children in 1998. By the end of the twentieth century, Mexico's air quality had declined from an average visibility of 62 miles in the 1940s to only 1 mile in 2000. Ozone content exceeded safe levels 97 percent of the days in the 1990s. How did Mexico become so polluted in such a short period of time? The geography of Mexico City contributes to the manmade factors that led to this severe environmental state of affairs. The altitude of Mexico City, averaging 7,347 feet, means that the oxygen content at that altitude is approximately one-fourth less than found at sea level. Residents breathe more deeply to compensate for this oxygen differential, thus inhaling more pollutants. This "thinner" air also means the fossil fuels burn less efficiently. The metropolitan area also is geographically located in a large valley surrounded by higher mountain ranges that trap man-made pollutants. This produces what might be described as a giant bowl with an atmospheric cover.

Dramatic man-made changes exaggerated the impact of such natural climatic and geographic conditions. The city's metropolitan population increased from approximately three million in 1950 to 21 million by 2009. Mexicans drive four million vehicles daily, and they account for 70 to 80 percent of all emissions in the city. It was not until 1989 that Mexico City first introduced emissions tests. These tests led to a ban on people driving older cars one day a week, removing 320,000 cars weekly. On days of high pollution, such cars can be banned for a second day and some manufacturing activities are eliminated. Thirty percent of Mexico's industrial output is concentrated in the metropolitan and surrounding areas. Since 1990, Mexico City's highly successful program has been able to reduce lead levels by 95 percent, sulfur dioxide by 86 percent, and carbon monoxide by 74 percent.

Recent studies suggest that to further reduce the consequences of air pollution the city should concentrate on eliminating particulates of less than 10 micrometers. For example, a 10 percent reduction of these particulates would translate into 33,000 fewer emergency room visits in 2010 and 4,200 fewer hospital visits for respiratory ailments. The city's successful program has been emulated in other major metropolitan areas, but the city will have to expand its efforts to continue to further reduce deaths and illnesses attributed to air pollution.

How has Mexico addressed domestic and cross-border environmental issues?

Mexico faces numerous environmental issues internally and along the border. The major problems, regardless of location, include air pollution, hazardous waste, erosion, chemical contamination, clean water, sewage treatment, and misuse of pesticides. The democratic transformation in the 1990s contributed to the development of numerous nongovernmental organizations that focus on all aspects of environmental issues from maintaining and protecting ecological sites to eliminating air pollution. Those groups have increased public attention on these issues and made it possible for certain achievements in protecting the environment, most notably the air pollution program in Mexico City. In the political arena, Mexico created its own green party, the Green Ecological Party of Mexico (PVEM), which has come under the leadership of a single political family. Surveys demonstrate that Mexicans are not only aware of serious ecological threats, but also support actions to eliminate global warming and other long-term national environmental issues. President Calderón has made policies to reduce global warming a special and personal issue of his administration.

In spite of the attention that has been given to such issues, Mexico continues to face serious environmental challenges, largely because even when antipollution legislation exists, much of it is not being applied and enforced. Studies also show that degradation continued to occur because appropriate mechanisms for controlling economic growth in line with environmental standards were not in place in the 1990s and 2000s. The U.S. Environmental Protection Agency, in describing the 2012 U.S.-Mexico Border Program, suggested that the fourteen metropolitan areas along the border have abysmal air and water quality. The reasons for these conditions include rapid demographic growth in urban centers, poorly planned development, increased waste and unavailable treatment facilities, illegal dumping, poor agricultural drainage, airborne pesticides, and degradation of natural resources.

When the United States and Mexico joined forces to address environmental issues along the border in 1996, 88 percent of households in Mexico had potable water, 69 percent were connected to sewers, and 34 percent were using sewers with wastewater treatment facilities. By 2000, those figures had already improved to 93, 75, and 75 percent. Some of these projects have been funded by the North American Development Bank. The Border 2012 Program is highlighting an improved capacity to monitor and gather data on human exposure in the border region and to improve the border infrastructure to attack these problems. Mexico has also begun working closely with the United States since 2006 to develop renewable energy sources that can be consumed both in Mexico and in the United States. Another priority is to increase hazardous waste facilities equal in capacity to the wastes being generated. Mexico continues to face numerous challenges to improving its environmental conditions internally and along the border.

3

MEXICO'S POLITICAL DEVELOPMENT

When did Mexico become democratic?

When countries begin a process of changing from one political model to another, it can occur quickly or slowly, and can be brought about peacefully or violently. Mexico evolved under a political model that can be described as having been semi-authoritarian from the 1920s through 2000. Most theorists use several types of conditions to describe whether or not a country has become democratic. Typically, the most important variable that appears in almost everyone's definition of democracy is free, fair, and competitive elections. By that definition alone, it could be argued that Mexico had achieved some form of democracy, what can better be labeled electoral democracy, after the 1994 presidential election. The election itself, taking place under newly enforced electoral laws, was viewed as fair, even though some of the conditions under which the opposition parties competed against the long-time incumbent party, the Institutional Revolutionary Party (PRI), were not equitable. A more precise definition of electoral democracy, however, suggests that a country has reached that stage when the incumbent party, which in this case had been in power for seventy-one years, loses to an opposing party, which occurred in the 2000 presidential election with the victory of the National Action Party candidate, Vicente Fox.

President Ernesto Zedillo, the victor in 1994, helped to contribute to an environment, building on significant electoral reforms in 1996, that assured that the 2000 election would be fair in nearly all respects.

Despite these achievements, which occurred incrementally and largely without violence, Mexico should be described as an electoral democracy rather than a democracy per se. Other conditions that remain to be met or are not fully implemented would include the protection of human rights, a strong and equitable legal system, freedom of speech and press, transparency, and other characteristics linked to social justice. Mexico can best be described as in the process of democratic consolidation. In other words, it has not fully implemented many of the features that are associated with liberal democracy in other countries. For example, although investigative journalism has increased dramatically since 2000, contributing positively to civic support for democratic norms and processes, journalists investigating drug cartels repeatedly have been assassinated and threatened. Consequently most reporters can no longer sign stories involving serious investigations of the drug cartels, nor can they carry out intensive research on drug traffickers. Mexico continues to achieve other components of democracy, but it remains at the building stage to date.

How democratic is Mexico?

In answering the question in this chapter as to when Mexico became democratic, it was suggested that democratic theorists typically point to a number of conditions or characteristics that are generally associated with a functioning democratic model. Mexico only meets some of these criteria. These criteria include civilian supremacy over the military, competitive elections, participation of the citizenry in the political process, legitimacy of the legal system, protection of human rights, and the achievement of social justice. Mexico has most closely achieved a democratic political system in terms of the competitiveness of elections at both the local and national levels. Election results since 2000 have demonstrated the level of competitiveness. In the 2000 presidential race, for example, the National Action Party (PAN) defeated the long-time incumbent Institutional Revolutionary Party (PRI), which came in second, and the Party of the Democratic Revolution (PRD), which was a distant third place. In 2006, the PAN was barely able to retain its control of the executive branch by defeating the second strongest party, the PRD, by a half of one percent of the vote. In early 2011, a year and a half before the next presidential election, early polls suggest that the PRI is once again in the lead, and if the election were held in 2011, the PRI would easily defeat the PAN and the PRD. Well-run elections, overseen by a federal electoral institute and court, in combination with public financing, have leveled the playing field for the major parties. One criticism of the electoral process is that it remains too restrictive in precluding independent candidates from running for the presidency.

Another measure of Mexico's degree of democracy is civilian supremacy over the military. Civilian authorities do exercise decision-making control over most aspects of the armed forces' missions, but they have continued to allow the military autonomy in arresting, trying, and convicting its own members for human rights violations against civilians. Given the number of allegations against the military for such violations, critics point out that the rate of arrests and convictions is extraordinarily low. The question of ultimate civilian control over the military is also associated with another important test of Mexico's democratic achievements, the protection of human rights. Since 2000, the number of alleged human rights abuses has increased significantly, including those committed by the armed forces. The inability of the government to prevent or reduce these abuses, and its failure to thoroughly investigate and convict civilian and military perpetrators of such abuses extending back to Mexico's own Dirty War in the

1970s, suggests democratic limitations based on this measurement.

The government's degree of tolerance toward human rights abuses is also associated with the strength and functioning of Mexico's legal system. To their credit, Mexican states are now undergoing the implementation of reforms to the legal system that would help eliminate the widespread practice in the Mexican justice system of torturing the accused and relying exclusively on forced confessions to convict arrested suspects. To date, however, these legal reforms have not been fully tested in practice, nor has the public become convinced that they are protected under the legal system. Mexico as a democracy still has to achieve a reputable status for the culture of law.

Why did Mexico make the democratic transition so slowly?

When the Soviet Union collapsed, and the Eastern European countries began a transition to democracy, a similar pattern was occurring elsewhere in the world, especially in Latin America. Most Latin American countries that had suffered under repressive, authoritarian military regimes had achieved electoral democracies by the 1980s. Yet Mexico, next door to the most influential democracy in the world, continued its semi-authoritarian model. Mexico did not follow the chronological pattern found elsewhere in the region for several important reasons.

In the first place, countries such as Brazil, Chile, and Argentina, which achieved democratic electoral status in the 1980s, were returning to an existing model of democratic politics. In Mexico, however, competitive electoral politics made only the briefest of appearances in 1911, when Francisco Madero was elected to the presidency. Therefore, few if any Mexicans in the 1980s or 1990s had any memory, let alone personal experience with a democratic electoral process. A second explanation is that Mexico had been ruled by an incumbent party and interchangeable elite for seven decades. The continuity and stability of that incumbent leadership contributed to the difficulty of altering it through opposition politics. It also made large numbers of Mexicans fearful of undergoing a change in spite of the fact that the majority of voters had become increasingly critical of the PRI and its leaders. In other words, despite the leadership's numerous weaknesses, many Mexicans were afraid to try an alternative leadership. This resistance to change became known in Mexican politics as the "fear factor." It should be remembered that in the first honest election at the polling places, despite the largest turnout in Mexican history, Ernesto Zedillo, the PRI candidate, won the election with 49 percent of the vote, defeating the PAN, which obtained 26 percent. The Catholic Church can be given partial credit for helping Mexicans overcome those fears by explicitly encouraging voters to choose whichever party they preferred and specifically condemning any candidates who campaigned on the fear issue. In 2000, Vicente Fox won with 43 percent of the vote, defeating the PRI, which captured 33 percent of the ballots. A third of Mexican voters continued to support the party that had used a semi-authoritarian model to remain in power.

Finally, when Carlos Salinas became president in 1988, after winning a highly contested election marked by fraud, he decided to pursue a global economic strategy to improve Mexico's economic growth. He believed he could use economic success to continue his party's presence while retaining most of the authoritarian features it used prior to 1998. Ironically, voting patterns demonstrated that more economically developed urban locales increasingly voted against the PRI, while the poorest, rural regions continued to support the PRI.

What can Mexico teach us about civil-military relations?

One of the political conditions that has plagued most of Latin America in the twentieth century is the direct involvement of the armed forces in political affairs. Most militaries in the region have taken over directly their respective governments at some time since the 1950s, or have exercised control over civilian leadership. Mexico, however, has been a notable exception since the 1930s. After the Mexican revolution of 1910, with the exception of presidents Francisco Madero, Venustiano Carranza, and Emilio Portes Gil, all the presidents from 1911 to 1946 were generals who had fought in the revolution. A group of those leading veterans as well as some prominent civilians under the leadership of ex-president Plutarco Elias Calles, created a political organization, the National Revolutionary Party (PNR), in 1928–29, to unify the post-revolutionary leadership.

The PNR became a central vehicle for establishing a strong civilian leadership, a leadership which could compete effectively with an aging group of ambitious generals who wanted to continue their influence in Mexico's political process. After General Lázaro Cárdenas became president in 1934, he believed the most effective means of subordinating the army to civilian leadership was to incorporate members of the armed forces formally into the party as one of its four supporting sectors. His philosophy could be described as keeping the military formally in politics is the best way of preventing them from controlling the political system. His successor, however, and the last military president in Mexico, General Manuel Avila Camacho, reversed Cárdenas' strategy, eliminating the military sector from the party altogether, restricting military officers from direct involvement in electoral politics without permission from the secretary of national defense. Instead, selected officers were nominated for congressional and senate seats, and a number of career officers continued to serve as governors. From a financial perspective, federal expenditures for the armed forces declined significantly over time and eventually plummeted to a percentage (of the total budget) among the bottom third of all countries. From the 1920s through the 1940s, the officer corps was professionalized through intense training at the Heroic Military College, which socialized career officers to give absolute loyalty to their superiors and to their commander in chief, the president of Mexico.

After 1946, the civilian and military leadership evolved an unwritten arrangement in which the armed forces unquestionably subordinated itself and its missions to civilian leadership while accepting only modest increases in personnel and materiel. In exchange, the armed forces leadership was permitted to exercise considerable autonomy within its ranks, including trying its own members for legal infractions, crimes, and human rights abuses and allocating its federal budget for specific uses within the armed forces. By sacrificing control over those decisions, civilian leadership prevented military involvement in the general decision-making process for the rest of the century, firmly establishing an unbroken pattern of military subordination to civilian rule.

Why has Mexico been so stable since the 1930s?

When scholars compare Mexico with all other Third World countries, one of the universal conclusions they reach is how politically stable Mexico has been for most of the twentieth century. Mexico achieved that remarkable degree of stability for several reasons. In the first place, many political historians attribute the country's stability in part to the violent revolution it underwent during the second decade of the twentieth century. So many Mexicans were directly affected by that violent decade or participated personally in the revolution, that these collective experiences influenced their attitudes toward political violence and peaceful political development. An entire generation of Mexicans from the 1890s and 1900s who survived these events wanted to achieve political peace. That desire made them overly receptive to supporting political stability and continuity and willing to accept other features of the political system they found to be offensive.

Mexicans also wanted to develop an emphasis on civilian leadership after the 1920s, given the prior dominance of military politicians from the late 1870s through the 1930s. A younger generation of civilian politicians who came to power in the 1940s sacrificed the democratic political goals of the revolution, including effective suffrage, to strengthen their control over ambitious generals and other competitors, and to maintain that control through the remainder of the twentieth century. This younger civilian generation also presided over a period of sustained economic growth from the 1940s through the 1960s, giving the political leadership room to maneuver and an opportunity to consolidate its control and improve its techniques for dominating the political landscape.

The most important institutional political contributor to sustaining that stability was the emergence of the National Revolutionary Party in 1929, which eventually became the Institutional Revolutionary Party (PRI). The government and party leaders were able to maintain their dominance and control over the electoral process and national leadership in all three branches of government as well as among state governors until the 1990s. Mexican political leadership affiliated with this party was successful in achieving this goal because they were pragmatic in orientation, welcomed ambitious, younger politicians from both the ideological left and the right, and actively recruited talented figures in secondary, preparatory, and university environments. Each generation of politicians mentored a younger generation, contributing to an incremental quality in their personnel, while introducing new blood to each successive generation. Eventually, within its own ranks, an increasing number of politicians became disenchanted with the governing elite either because they were left out of the decision-making process, or truly wanted a more open and decentralized process for selecting future leaders. They abandoned this incumbent coalition, effectively challenging that leadership for control under the Party of the Democratic Revolution (PRD) and the National Action Party in 1988 and 1994, finally wresting it from the incumbent leaders in the 2000 presidential election. Nevertheless, these challenges occurred in the electoral arena and Mexico made the transition to electoral democracy with little violence and continued stability.

What is the impact of the United States on Mexico's political development and democratization?

People often wonder when they examine the geographic proximity of Mexico to the United States to what degree its northern neighbor influenced the pace and direction of Mexico's political development. The U.S. government has involved itself in Mexican political affairs on numerous occasions, including overtly during the Mexican-American War of 1846, the occupation of Veracruz in 1914, and the extended pursuit of Pancho Villa in northern Mexico in 1916, and through indirect pressure on Mexican foreign policy positions and its transition to democracy. For most of the second half of the twentieth century, as was true elsewhere in the region, the U.S. government was more interested in a country's political stability than in the level of pluralism in its politics. Until the end of the 1970s, the United States did little to encourage Mexico's leadership or its opposition critics to move in the direction of a democratic political model.

In the 1980s, when Jesse Helms was the ranking Republican on the U.S. Senate Foreign Relations Committee, and from 1995–2001, when he chaired the committee, the legislative branch began using legislative hearings under the auspices of the subcommittee on the Western Hemisphere as a means of creating public pressure on Mexican leadership to move the country toward competitive, democratic elections. Such fair elections were first tried locally under President Miguel de la Madrid in 1983, resulting in seven major victories for the National Action Party in important municipalities. Their success so stunned the government that the incumbent leadership persuaded the president to return to PRI electoral practices as usual. The efforts of Helms produced more influential consequences after Carlos Salinas de Gortari was elected in a fraud-plagued race in 1988. When President Salinas joined President Bush in an effort to negotiate a three-way trade agreement among Mexico, Canada, and the United States, Helms used the Mexican government's overwhelming desire to consummate such an agreement as a means of increasing the pressure for democratic elections.

In spite of such pressures emanating from the U.S. legislative branch, the executive branch exercised little or no influence on Mexico's transition to democracy. If any influence on the direction of Mexico's political development can be attributed to the United States, it most likely can be identified with the elite media and nongovernmental organizations. The media, particularly the *Los Angeles Times*, the *New York Times*, the *Dallas Morning News*, and the *Wall Street Journal* exerted significant influence on the country's political development through its critical coverage and editorials. For example, President Salinas annulled the 1991 election results for governor of Guanajuato after a *Wall Street Journal* editorial criticized it for fraud, believing that this newspaper's opinion staunchly reflected that of Wall Street and that Wall Street was an essential ally in obtaining United States support for NAFTA. Furthermore, the media began publishing its own public opinion polls that, similar to Mexican polls, could confirm actual voter preferences in comparison to the government reported returns. NGOs in the United States also collaborated closely with their counterparts in Mexico, including their participation as election observers, a critical contributor to forcing the Mexican government into carrying out fair elections.

4

FOREIGN RELATIONS WITH THE UNITED STATES

What is the impact of geography on Mexico?

Mexico's proximity to the United States has exerted an extraordinary influence on Mexico economically, politically and culturally. The two countries share a 1,954-mile border. The disparity in the level of income between the two countries has produced numerous consequences. Perhaps the most important of these consequences has been the economic influence exerted by the United States on Mexico's economic development in the nineteenth and twentieth centuries. During the reign of Porfirio Díaz, from 1884 to 1910, U.S. investment and involvement in numerous sectors of the economy, including mining, railroads, and petroleum, allowed private actors to exert inordinate influence on political and economic matters. No better example of that exists than the ability of the owners of the Cananea Consolidated Copper Co. to request that Arizona Rangers cross the border during a major strike against the company in June 1906, illustrating a flagrant violation of Mexican territorial sovereignty. In the twentieth century, Mexico became the United States' second most important trading partner after Canada (recently trading places back and forth with China), whereas the United States remains Mexico's most important trading partner, suggesting how geographic proximity has encouraged those commercial influences. But beyond the direct foreign investment and the magnitude of two countries' trade relations, Mexican immigration to the United States, the most significant of any country in the world, is the product of that very proximity, as for decades Mexicans have sought economic opportunities in the United States. Beyond the level of illegal immigration and the multitude of contemporary social and political issues it generates, Mexico and the United States share the largest exchange of citizens in the world. It is now estimated that between six hundred thousand and one million Americans live in Mexico. (See Table 2 for how this proximity has affected Mexican and American views of each other.)

The geographic proximity between the two countries historically has led to multiple conflicts, of which the most significant was the Mexican-American War of 1846, when Mexico lost much of its national territory to the United States. These historical encounters led to a strong sense of Mexican nationalism toward the United States. Only in recent years, reflected in the willingness of the majority of Mexicans to join in a free trade agreement with the United States, has Mexico tempered its nationalistic views toward its northern neighbor. Beyond the more traditional political consequences that geography can have on such a relationship, the cultural influences have been extraordinary. Given the asymmetry between the two countries, and the extensive musical, literary, artistic, and other cultural influences the United States has exerted globally, it is not surprising that such cultural influences in Mexico are pronounced. On the other hand, in the last two decades, the level of cultural influence exerted by Mexico in the United States has grown significantly, especially when examining the impact of Mexican cuisine, popular music, and language. Spanish is the most widely taught language in the United States, in no small part due to Mexico's proximity and the numbers of Americans who travel to Mexico.

Table 2 How Mexicans and Americans view each other, 2006

	Mexican %	American %
Question	Agree with the statement	
Favorable impression of Americans/Mexicans	35	85
Favorable impression of American/Mexican government	27	27
Mexicans are very hard-working.	49	53
Americans are very hard-working.	11	21
Mexicans are tolerant.	74	76
Americans are tolerant.	43	79
Mexicans are law-abiding.	71	71
Americans are law-abiding.	62	91
Mexicans are racists.	49	50
Americans are racists.	73	35
Migrant workers benefit U.S. economy.	80	67
Mexican are discriminated against in the United States.	80	73
Democracy more important than effective government	63	62
Distant neighbor best describes how United States sees Mexico.	36	49
Which language is the best second language, English/Spanish?	89	78
Cultural impact of Mexico on United States favorable	40	43
Cultural impact of United States on Mexico favorable	21	48
Would you approve of your child marrying American/Mexican?	52	81
Community is more important than the individual.	69	72

Source: Encuesta CIDAC-ZOGBY Mexico y Estados Unidos, "Como miramos al vecino," 2006.

What has happened with immigration to the United States?

Mexican migration to the United States boasts a long history extending back more than a century. Immigrants have crossed the northern border for political reasons, especially during the Mexican Revolution of 1910, but typically for economic reasons, in search of a better standard of living. Today, the Mexican-born population in the United States totals nearly 11.5 million, five times as many migrants as from any other country. Of those individuals, approximately 59 percent are undocumented immigrants. As of 2008, 10 percent of the U.S. population was of Mexican origin and 15 percent of Hispanic origin. Two thirds of all Hispanics in the United States are of Mexican origin. The dramatic increase in the Mexican-born population has occurred since World War II, and especially since the 1980s, when Mexicans went from 12 percent of the foreign born-population to 30 percent in 2008.

The extent of Mexican immigration in the last decade has become a volatile domestic policy issue because of the size of the undocumented population, the fact that most Mexicans physically cross the border between the two countries, and the economic impact of the largest concentration of immigrants on numerous services in local communities, especially health and education. The economic recession in 2008 introduced other factors, including the perception by many working Americans that immigrants are taking away jobs. Symbolically and disproportionately, undocumented immigrants as a source of crime also impacts on public opinion even if in reality federal statistics do not support these perceptions. The largest concentrations of Mexican immigrants can be found in California, Texas, Arizona, and Illinois. Indeed, the largest concentration of Mexicans outside Mexico is located in Los Angeles. Since 2000, however, undocumented immigrants can be found in increasing numbers in nearly every state.

Most serious observers of undocumented immigration agree that immigration reform is critical. The majority of Americans also agree with the need for immigration reform. In fact, according to a *New York Times* poll in April–May 2010, only 24 percent of younger Americans between the ages of 18 and 44 favored reducing immigration. Laws governing immigration have remained largely unchanged since the mid-1960s. President George W. Bush intended to introduce immigration reform in Congress, but his efforts were derailed by the September 11 terrorist attacks. The fundamental weakness of current immigration laws are that few individuals are able to come to the United States temporarily or permanently for work-related reasons. Statistics from Homeland Security in 2009 revealed that 66 percent of all new legal permanent residents obtained residency based on family ties, while only 13 percent did so through employment-based preferences.

Contrary to what many Americans believe, when the U.S. economy declines, the number of Mexican immigrants also declines. Typically, critics identify the economic costs of undocumented migrants without mentioning their economic contributions. In short, poorly paid migrant labor work extensively in numerous urban services and construction and in the agricultural sector. The cost of vegetables, fruits, poultry, and other food products for all Americans, for example, is subsidized by the low cost of hundreds of thousands of Mexican migrant workers, documented and undocumented, who are employed in these and other important economic sectors. Mexican migrants, through economic remittances sent back to their families in Mexico exceeding $21 billion yearly since 2005, also are contributing directly and significantly to the economic development of their country of origin, which in the long run will reduce migration to the United States. The passage of a controversial immigration bill in Arizona in 2010 is a consequence in large part of Congress's failure to address immigration reform and to educate themselves and their constituencies about the complexities, both positive and negative, of undocumented immigration.

Could the International Boundary and Water Commission serve as an institutional model for other issues with the United States?

Many of the intractable issues that have existed in the relationship between Mexico and the United States have been on the bilateral agenda for more than half a century. One of the most difficult of those issues, which has received little attention in the media, in Congress, or among the general public, is the sharing of water resources, namely from the Rio Grande and Colorado rivers, as well as the changing boundaries of the Rio Grande (Rio Bravo in Mexico). The Rio Grande extends the entire length of the Texas-Mexico border, and the Colorado flows between Baja California and Sonora, where it used to empty into the Sea of Cortez—before huge amounts of water were drawn from the river by metropolitan water districts in California, Nevada, and Arizona. Water issues, contrary to what most Americans might think, are complex, significant, and involve numerous actors, local, state, and federal. The International Boundary and Water Commission traces its history back to the second half of the nineteenth century to the establishment of the Boundary Commission in 1889. This commission was created to solve boundary issues resulting from the Rio Grande changing its course. The growth of border populations on both sides of the river in the twentieth century and the expansion of agriculture required decisions to be made about the allocation of water to both countries. Over the years, the level of salinity in the water increased due to repeated agricultural use in the upper regions of both rivers in the United States. This situation also required complex negotiations to prevent the water from being unusable by the time it reached the lower portions of the river. At the end of World War II, in 1944, the commission was given its current name and became responsible for interpreting and applying all water treaties between the two nations. The most well-known issue resolved by the commission was that of the El Chamizal dispute between Ciudad Juárez, Chihuahua, and El Paso, Texas, which arose when more than 600 acres of land transferred from one side to the other as a consequence of the changing river channel.

The commission is divided into two organizations on both sides of the border. These counterpart organizations consist of administrative and engineering units, and are headed by a commissioner with diplomatic status. During the last five decades they have developed an enviable, long-term relationship based on objective and careful technical information, resolving issues that have local, practical, and domestic consequences, efficiently and satisfactorily. As border issues increase in number and difficulty, the success of the commission offers insights into how other comparable bilateral organizations might be structured and staffed to deal with environmental and other complex problems, including undocumented immigration.

What can the United States do to help Mexico?

Although numerous ways exist in which the United States could help Mexico, by far the most important assistance our country can give to Mexico is economic. Despite the media's intense focus on the level of violence in Mexico and the drug war strategy that has promoted that response, Mexico's most important national security issue, both for Mexico and for the United States, is poverty. For Mexico to successfully reduce poverty and to increase its economic growth, it has to take numerous steps that only it alone can take. Nevertheless, the United States can help Mexico implement such policies more effectively and/or allow it to redirect scarce resources to those programs that have proven most successful in addressing poverty.

The single most important contribution the United States can make to Mexico's economic development is to get its own economic house in order and to pursue a continuous, steady rate of economic growth over a long period of time. Because of the trade ties introduced by the North American Free Trade Agreement in 1994, Mexico has become increasingly dependent on trade with the United States as a source of its economic growth and its foreign capital investment. A recession in the United States affects Mexico's economy more than that of any of the United States' other important trading partners.

A second policy the United States should consider adopting is to increase economic assistance to Mexico, especially allocating funds to supplement Mexico's own efforts to reduce poverty in programs like Oportunidades. Mexico has increased its antipoverty programs since 2000, but given its limited federal revenues, the adverse effects of the 2008 recession, and the increased expenditures on national security in fighting organized crime, it needs more revenues assigned to that task. What assistance the United States does provide to Mexico has largely been security related. Furthermore, if Mexico could increase economic growth, personal income, and employment opportunities, it would reduce the appeal of growing drugs and working for drug cartels.

Third, the United States could contribute significantly to Mexico's economic growth, and its ability to attract new investment, by radically reducing its demand for drugs. As President Barack Obama's drug czar indicated in an interview in 2009, if his agency received an additional $10 billion dollars, he would spend the entire amount on drug prevention and education, not on interdiction. The violence and the economic consequences of that violence and the strength of organized crime is largely a product of drug habits in the United States. Few investors want to risk their monies in economic opportunities where violence is rampant and government sovereignty is in question.

Finally, the United States needs to take the initiative with Mexico to produce immigration reform. Mexico is losing its most creative workforce to economic opportunities in the United States. By legalizing immigration and providing documented workers temporary opportunities, the United States would also contribute to alleviating poverty in Mexico, both by employing migrants and teaching them new skills, and providing a source of direct foreign investment through migrant remittances. Remittances have become the second most important source of foreign revenues after petroleum. Recipients of remittances, 83 percent of which come from undocumented workers according to the Bank of Mexico, spend nearly four-fifths of that income on housing, food, and utilities, and 7 percent on education. In 2008, remittances accounted for 2.4 percent of Mexico's GDP.

How has Mexico influenced the United States economically?

Mexico has played a significant role in the rapid expansion of United States exports in the 1990s and 2000s. Mexico has alternated between the second and third most important trade partner of the United States in the last decade. In 2009, the United States exported a total of $129 billion worth of goods to Mexico, the most important of these products coming from computers and electronics, transportation, and machinery sectors. Canada purchased 19 percent of our exports in 2009, followed by Mexico, which accounted for 12 percent. China only purchased 7 percent of U.S. exports. Exports to Mexico accounted for approximately 759,000 jobs in the United States in 2009. California alone, boasting the eighth largest economy in the world, exports more than 15 percent of its products to Mexico, exceeding what it trades with Canada, Japan, and China. As of 2005, Mexico's purchases of California exports supported nearly 200,000 jobs in the state. In fact, 17 percent of all export-supported jobs in California, which account for a fifth of all individuals employed in the state, are linked to the state's economic relationship with Mexico. More than half of those export-related positions can be traced to the North American Free Trade Agreement. California and Texas, the two largest economies in the United States, which are two of the three largest state/provincial economies in the world, are significantly influenced economically by Mexico. Six states, in 2009, Texas (34 percent), Arizona (32 percent), New Mexico (30 percent), New Hampshire (25 percent), South Dakota (23 percent), and Nebraska (23 percent), depend heavily on Mexico to purchase their exports. The GDP of the U.S. and Mexican border states accounts for a fourth of the national economy of both countries combined, exceeding the GDP of all the countries in the world except for the United States, Japan, China, and Germany.

The United States provides the single largest amount of direct foreign investment in Mexico, but Mexican entrepreneurs and venture capitalists invest in the United Sates. In California by 2000, for example, Mexicans owned firms in the state worth $1.1 billion and employed 9,700 residents. By 2008, Mexico was investing $7.9 billion in the United States, exceeding the level of direct foreign investments from economies as large as Germany and India, much of it along the southwest border. Finally, Mexico also influences the U.S. economy through tourism in the same way that American tourists play a central role in Mexico's economy. In 2009, 55 million foreigners visited the United States, generating $94 billion dollars. Canada accounts for the largest number of visitors each year, followed by Mexico, which provided ten million tourists as early as 2000. Along the border, at the end of the decade, Mexican visitors generated some $8 billion to $9 billion dollars in sales and supported approximately 150,000 jobs. The number of individuals who cross the southwest border into Mexico for short visits far exceeds the total number of tourists. Pedestrians from Mexico have exceeded 45 million a year since 1999, and those traveling by car have reached more than 75 million since 1997.

5

MEXICO'S SOCIAL DEVELOPMENT

How unequal is Mexican development and what are the social consequences?

Mexico's development, depending on the measurement used, is considered to be significantly unequal, as is Latin American as a whole the most unequal region in the world. Levels of inequality typically are measured economically, most commonly according to one's level of income. The most well-known of those economic measures is the Gini coefficient. When Mexico is compared with other middle-income economies, it ranks among the most unequal along with Russia and Estonia. In income inequality, Mexico ranks about the same as the United States on the Gini scale. Recent studies have argued that other measures provide more accurate and subtle measurements of inequality. For example, to what extent is Mexico characterized by inequality in opportunity? Other combined measures of quality of life scales have included such variables as access to services such as water or health care.

Studies by economists have shown definitively that economic inequality is linked to inequalities in water supply, drainage, and other basic structures such as housing. It also affects access to electricity, but to a lesser extent than other variables. Inequality, no matter how it is measured, affects the geography of poverty. The effects of inequality also are much more dramatic in rural than in urban areas. Indeed, the consequences of inequality in Mexico decrease significantly in urban locales. Mexico boasts some of the most developed municipalities in the world according to the United Nations Human Development Report, while at the same time it includes municipalities that are ranked lower than those found in sub-Saharan Africa. The ten lowest ranking municipalities out of a study of more than two thousand municipalities in Mexico typically were found in poor, rural states such as Oaxaca, Chiapas, and Guerrero, all of which are located in southern Mexico, a region long viewed as Mexico's poorest, while the north is recognized as the wealthiest region.

In addition to geographical inequities, which have existed for decades, these economic inequalities are associated with race and ethnicity. The three states mentioned above are among those with the highest percentage of indigenous Mexicans. Indigenous Mexicans not only receive lower incomes, live in poorer housing, and share less access to services, but are less likely to complete elementary school, to be literate, to speak Spanish fluently, and to develop the skills necessary to improve their family's economic situation. For example, 24.6 percent of indigenous Mexicans compared with 6.4 percent of the nonindigenous Mexicans are illiterate. Inequality also affects trust and political participation. Social capital, the willingness of people to become involved in their societies as active citizens, is also linked to social inequality and the low levels of trust toward fellow citizens and institutions among those at the bottom of the economic and social ladder.

What is the current status of indigenous Mexicans?

The Mexican government recognizes sixty-four different indigenous ethnicities, accounting for 13.9 million inhabitants, approximately 12 percent of the current population. When Mexico achieved independence, indigenous people accounted for approximately 60 percent of all Mexicans, and by the 1900s, they had declined to only 37 percent. Given Mexico's rapid rate of demographic growth in the twentieth century, however, the absolute numbers of indigenous Mexicans today exceeds the total at the time of the 1910 Revolution. Nearly half of the indigenous population speaks a native dialect, while nearly 90 percent speak both Spanish and their native language. The percentage of indigenous Mexicans who speak a native dialect varies widely depending on the language spoken. For example, Nahuatl and Maya are the most widely spoken languages, but fewer than 10 percent speak those languages exclusively. In contrast, more than a fourth of Tzeltal and Tzotzil speakers (typically from Chiapas) only speak their indigenous language. Seven out of ten indigenous Mexicans live in indigenous communities. Those states with the largest indigenous populations are Oaxaca, Chiapas, Veracruz, and Yucatán. However, those states with the highest concentration of native speakers are Chiapas and Guerrero, where they account for nearly a fourth of the residents, followed by Oaxaca, Durango, and Hidalgo.

Indigenous people are among the poorest of all Mexicans, regardless of the measure used. In terms of income, approximately 20 percent of Mexicans over the age of 12 living in mestizo communities received no income compared with 31 percent who resided in predominantly indigenous municipalities. Two-fifths of Mexicans received the equivalent of, or more than, a minimum salary, compared with only one-fourth of those from indigenous communities. The average speaker of a native language has completed only four and a half years of education, while 70 percent have access to potable water, 54 percent to a sewage system, and 89 percent to electricity.

The uprising of indigenous Mexicans belonging to the Zapatista Army of National Liberation (popularly known as the Zapatistas), on January 1, 1994, focused significant attention on the plight of the indigenous population, especially in Chiapas. Also as a result of the Zapatista movement,

Congress granted new rights to all indigenous communities in Mexico focusing on self-governance. The federal government recommended that the states alter their constitutions to enhance these changes, but as of 2008, only four of thirty-two states and entities have introduced such alterations. Culturally, Mexico has taken great pride in the architecture and achievements of their indigenous cultures, as well as in their arts and crafts, highlighted in numerous museums, including the renowned National Museum of Anthropology and History in the capital. But as many of these statistics reveal, native peoples in Mexico have yet to share equally in the country's social and economic development, and they remain underrepresented politically in the national leadership.

What are Mexican attitudes toward global environmental issues?

One of the dramatic shifts in global attitudes beginning in the 1990s is how humans viewed environmental issues. Survey data from the first World Values Surveys in 1990 demonstrate this change, and more importantly suggest that many countries, including Mexico, are more strongly supportive of pro-environmental policies compared with U.S. citizens. For example, when Americans were asked if they would give part of their income to prevent pollution, 75 percent of all respondents said yes. In contrast, four out of five Mexicans answered positively, placing them in the top ten countries, equivalent to Sweden. A decade later, Mexican support essentially remained unchanged, but still well ahead of Americans. Two-thirds of Mexicans responded favorably when asked if they would agree with an increase in taxes if it would be used to prevent pollution. Americans ranked lower than Mexicans in their responses to the first question in 1990 and 2000, and to the second question only in 2000. Surprisingly, in a country with difficult economic problems and widespread poverty, more than half of all Mexicans agreed with the view that protecting the environment should be given priority over economic growth and creating jobs. That figure was equally true of low-income Mexicans, suggesting strongly entrenched views among all social classes favorable to environmental issues.

Surveys also reveal the extent to which Mexicans and others would be willing to join voluntary organizations that would promote conservation and environmental protections. The United States is characterized by one of the highest levels of participation generally in voluntary organizations. In the 1990s, 9 percent of Americans indicated they were members of an environmental organization, the case for 3 percent of Mexicans. Finally, six out of ten individuals worldwide strongly approve of ecology groups, while 70 percent of Mexicans supported such organizations compared with only 45 percent of Americans.

Mexico has created a number of environmental organizations in the last three decades, ranging from ones that protect botanical resources to ones that prevent all forms of pollution. Pronatura, founded in 1981, is by far the largest environmental group in Mexico. It is focused on protecting wildlife, wetlands, and other traditional conservation issues. It is represented in more than half of Mexico's states. Yet, in spite of NGO activity and governmental regulations, Mexico is losing an estimated .9 percent of its forests yearly. While public attitudes clearly favor environmental protections, most environmental laws are not enforced by the cabinet level agency in charge of these policies, and little evidence exists of corporate or individual compliance with most environmental regulations.

PART II

HISTORICAL LEGACIES

6

MEXICO'S COLONIAL HERITAGE

How did the Spanish viceroys shape Mexico's political heritage in the 19th and 20th centuries?

When Spain sent expeditions to what is today Mexico and conquered the indigenous populations, they needed to create a structure of governance for their colonies in North and South America. The Spanish crown, through a Council of the Indies, created a system based in part on their reconquest of Spain from the Moors. The most important institution in the Spanish New World was the viceroy, or vice king. Given that Spain governed territory from the Tierra del Fuego as far north as what is today Kansas, the task of governing was an immense challenge because of the difficulties of communication between Spain and the new world and within the entire North American continent. For more than a century, beginning in the 1500s, Spain divided the colonies into two viceroyalties, and Mexico was part of the viceroyalty of New Spain, which eventually included the Philippine Islands.

Under the Spanish system, the viceroy combined three major powers. He was the political leader of the entire territory encompassed by New Spain. In addition to having civil powers, he was also the commander in chief of the militia in the region. Finally, he was vice-patron of the Catholic Church.

By giving the viceroy such combined, extraordinary powers to govern, the crown created a political institution that concentrated most decision-making authority into the hands of one individual and created a system of governance that assigned to what could be described today as the executive branch most of the political, military, and, to a great degree, religious power. This pattern of governance, in spite of the presence of a weak legislative body as well as stronger, pluralistic local authorities, created a significant heritage during three centuries of colonial rule favoring a concentration of power in the executive branch. Considering that many of the organized indigenous cultures conquered by the Spanish also were governed by their quasi religious-political authoritarian structures, the combined European and indigenous heritage promoted an authoritarian, hierarchical experience superimposed on localized, semi-independent communities. The colonies remained divided into two major viceroyalties, New Spain, founded in 1535, and Peru, established in 1543, until New Granada was added in 1739 and Río de la Plata in 1776.

As is the case with most authoritarian political structures, such a concentration of power creates the potential for abuses of authority, and some later viceroys, many of whom served for long terms at the whim of the crown, were found to have been corrupt or to have abused their authority. These negative characteristics combined with the concentrated authority, in part, contributed to the colonists' growing dissatisfaction with colonial rule, eventually leading to independence movements in New Spain and elsewhere in the colonies. Nevertheless, in spite of Mexico achieving independence in 1821, its first leader, Agustin Iturbide, declared himself emperor, continuing the authoritarian tradition established by the long reign of viceroys.

In the remainder of the nineteenth century, except for a brief period in the 1860s and 1870s, Mexico's political system was dominated by strong individual rulers, who governed through their personalities rather than through institutions, contributing to the long-term weakness of established political structures. By the twentieth century, ordinary Mexicans rejected the most durable example of this centralized control, that of Porfirio Díaz, who ruled from 1884 to 1911. This rejection took the form of a violent revolution during the decade from 1910 to 1920. Despite this rejection of Díaz, and a political mantra of no reelection, Mexico evolved a political system after the 1920s that also relied on a centralized, authoritarian model, led by a collective leadership, and that produced a different president every six years. Revisionist scholarship in the last decade has demonstrated that many Mexicans, since independence, have expressed democratic values and attempted to put them into practice, especially at the local level.

What was the relationship between church and state in Mexico and why was it so different from that of the United States?

Unlike the United States, which was founded on the principle of religious freedom and the separation of church and state, Mexico's religious heritage was quite distinct. Beginning with the Spanish reconquest of Spain from the Moors between the 700s and the 1300s, the role of the Catholic Church as the sole representative of Christianity in Spain was essential. This experience influenced the Spanish Crown to assign the Catholic Church a fundamental role in the conquest of New Spain, a large part of which became Mexico in 1821. Beginning with the expeditions to the New World, the Crown assigned two priests to every land or sea expedition. Spanish authorities believed priests could be useful in facilitating the European conquest of the indigenous communities. Their belief proved to be accurate. Indeed, a case could be made that after the initial phase of the violent conquest by the soldiers, priests were essential to increasing the expansion of Spanish political authorities. Using their intellectual skills, they learned numerous indigenous languages and provided a liaison among soldiers, conquistadores, and the indigenous leaders.

The Spanish authorities created an ambitious mission system, operated by members of religious orders such as the Franciscans or Jesuits and designed to produce agricultural goods and products to benefit the Spanish economy. These missions existed throughout New Spain and eventually became the basis for numerous influential cities in the United States, including Albuquerque, Tucson, Los Angeles, San Diego, and San Francisco. Once the initial colonies were established, the Church was assigned the responsibility for being a censor of radical ideas, including religious beliefs which were viewed as heretical to Catholicism, such as Judaism, Protestantism, and indigenous religions, as well as radical secular beliefs questioning the authority of the monarchical system on which the colonial structure relied. The Church generated an index of banned books that were not allowed to circulate in the colonies and controlled the publication of political and religious tracts. Their representatives served as customs inspectors, along with civil officials, searching for such banned works on incoming ships.

Assigned these and other responsibilities, the Church, in effect, was an essential ally of the state in the New World. It supported the Crown and became an integral part of the governing structure. This does not mean, however, that their relationship did not involve tensions and conflicts. Over the centuries, for example, religious orders tried to retain long-term control over numerous mission properties, bringing them in conflict both with diocesan authorities, that is, ordinary priests, as well as civil authorities. They were given the responsibility of protecting the indigenous populations from exploitation by the colonists, but more typically Church representatives colluded with the settlers to exploit the indigenous people.

What consequences did the colonial relationship between church and state have for the 19th and 20th centuries?

For three centuries, the Spanish Crown and the Catholic Church collaborated in maintaining control of New Spain. Although uprisings occurred on the frontiers, for example, in Albuquerque, New Mexico, this collaboration was largely successful in maintaining order and control by civil authorities until the 1810s. After independence was achieved in 1821, Mexico began a search for a new political model to replace the Crown and the traditionally close collaboration between church and state. By the 1850s, Mexico's politically active population had evolved into two distinct ideological factions, the Liberals and the Conservatives. The Conservatives believed that in order for Mexico to develop, it needed to rely on a political model that would stress centralized authority, arguing that the Spanish authoritarian heritage, managed by Conservative politicians, would produce the best results. They thought that decentralized political authority, given Mexico's colonial heritage, was unworkable. As part of their argument, they believed that the Church should continue to exercise an important role in Mexico's social and political development, viewing it as an important political ally, particularly given the economic wealth of the Catholic Church. It is estimated to have owned nearly half of Mexico's real estate.

By contrast, the Liberals, influenced significantly by the experience of the United States, believed that a decentralized political model, assigning greater decision-making authority to the legislative branch, was essential to Mexico's political development. They went beyond this argument, however, to suggest that the economic, social, and political influence exercised by the Catholic Church was detrimental to Mexico's development. Therefore, they wanted to destroy the Church's influence in a variety of activities. The extreme differences in the way the Conservatives and Liberals viewed the Church's role in Mexico's future political model led to a civil war between the two groups. In the 1850s, after the Liberals finally defeated the Conservatives, they passed a number of laws, known as the Reform Laws, designed to permanently limit the Church's influence. These laws were incorporated in Mexico's 1857 Constitution, which remained in effect until 1917. They forced the Church to divest itself of its property and sell it on the open market. They also secularized cemeteries to prevent priests from collecting fees. These and other restrictions were designed to eliminate the Church's economic influence. The Liberals also believed that the Church exercised a pernicious influence on the population through their control over the educational system, which had been entirely in their hands. Consequently, Liberals also created a public elementary as well as a preparatory education system, and eliminated Church control over schools. The conflict between church and state became a central issue in the political development of Mexico in the 1850s and 1860s, and was revived again during and after the Mexican Revolution. In the 1917 Constitution, the restrictions were even more draconian, including preventing the Church from owning real property, priests and nuns from voting, and prohibiting priests from using the pulpit to express political views. The strict enforcement of such restrictions led to the Cristero Rebellion, when Mexicans in support of the Church bitterly fought federal troops from 1926 to 1929. Despite the removal of certain provisions governing religious behavior in the Constitution in 1992, some of the principles that restricted the role of the Catholic Church remain in effect to this day.

What is the most important heritage of Spain's economic system in Mexico?

The economic system characterizing New Spain during the three hundred years of colonial rule produced numerous economic and social consequences that influenced the political conflicts of the nineteenth century and Mexico's economic and social development through the beginning of the twentieth century. Perhaps the broadest single characteristic that can be traced back to the colonial economic heritage is the large role of the state and a weak private sector. The Crown, through the Council of the Indies and its succession of Viceroys, affected the economic and social development of hundreds of thousands of indigenous Mexicans. In assigning lands to individuals, typically from Spain, it established the preeminent role of governmental institutions in influencing the direction of economic development and favoring certain groups over others in the distribution of economic resources and favors. Similar concessions were repeated by President Porfirio Díaz during his 1884–1911 administration. These economic decisions also reinforced the significant social distinctions between indigenous residents and the vast majority of mestizo Mexicans on one hand and, on the other, those Mexicans solely of Spanish descent.

After independence, in the 1830s, the *peninsulares*, or Mexicans from Spain, and creoles, Mexicans of Spanish descent born in Mexico, controlled most of the landed wealth that was not owned by the Catholic Church, which is estimated to have owned half of the real estate in Mexico in that era. The limited ownership of most land among a small number of Mexicans and one corporate entity, the Church, limited the economic growth and expansion of the private sector. Most businesses employed family members in management positions, making it difficult for other Mexicans to achieve upward economic mobility through meritorious credentials and entrepreneurial ability. Those limiting characteristics impact Mexico's economic vitality and growth today, reflected in the fact that many of the most influential corporations remain controlled by small, extended families, limiting the expansion of public ownership. The slow growth of stock ownership among large numbers of Mexicans can be attributed in part to the weak role of the private sector after the Mexican Revolution and the traditions found in the pre-independence era.

How were social class relations determined by colonial experiences?

During the initial phase of Spanish colonization of New Spain, few Spanish women accompanied the expeditions. Later, the Crown actually encouraged wives and single women to go to the colonies, believing they were important to spreading Spanish culture in New Spain. During the actual conquest of the indigenous Mexicans, native leaders also gave their daughters as prospective wives to the Spanish leaders. These two conditions led to common-law unions throughout Mexico and altered the demographic composition of the Spanish New World. These unions set in motion the blending of the Spanish, indigenous, and Africans brought from the Caribbean into a mixed race known as mestizos. The mestizo population expanded rapidly and by the time of independence, accounted for more than half of the population. The Spaniards devised a complex description of the mixture (*castas*) among European, indigenous, and African, depending on the percentage (parts) of an individual's ancestry according to race. They eventually created dozens of racial categories ranked by social order, from lowest to highest.

As one might imagine, the Spaniards gave top preference to those Mexicans who came directly from Spain—that is, were born in Spain. These residents of New Spain were popularly known as peninsulares. The next highest social category were Mexicans of pure Spanish descent, but born in the New World. These individuals became known as creoles, that is Mexicans of European descent. The peninsulares were quite small in number given the fact that many of them represented one or two generations. The pure-blood creoles were more numerous, but in percentage terms also were quite small in numbers. The mestizos, originally consisting of Spaniards and Indians, eventually evolved into multiple mixtures of Creole, indigenous, and African. Finally, the indigenous and African groups ranked at the very bottom. These sharp social divisions, so strongly emphasized during the colonial era, shaped social class relations in the nineteenth and twentieth centuries.

When Mexico achieved independence, the Spaniards and the Creoles controlled most economic resources. Mexicans were strongly divided over the strategy they should pursue for their political and economic development, but the two leading parties, the Liberals and the Conservatives, were largely led and controlled by Creoles. It was not until the mid-nineteenth century that the mestizo class dominated the political and military leadership. Despite their influence in political matters, descendants of important Creole families, owners of large landed estates and businesses, often controlled or strongly influenced political leadership at the local and state level. The 1910 Revolution was fought in part by mestizos who wanted increased upward mobility not just in public life but also in the private sector. While indigenous Mexicans participated heavily in the revolution, and their culture received symbolic recognition after 1920, for the most part their lives did not improve materially or socially, and cultural racism continued unabated.

7

THE NATIONAL PERIOD AND THE RISE OF LIBERAL-CONSERVATIVE CONFLICTS

What are the long-term consequences of Liberal-Conservative conflicts in Mexico?

The Liberal-Conservative conflict that emerged in Mexico after the 1830s reflects a pattern found in many other countries in South and Central America during the nineteenth century. Basically, these two parties represented opposing political and economic views as to how Mexico should be governed, and how it should best pursue economic and social development. There were two major ideological preferences differentiating Liberals from Conservatives in Mexico, which produced serious consequences affecting Mexico in the twentieth century. The most important political argument between these two parties focused on whether Mexico could be governed best under a political model that concentrated power in the hands of a strong executive leader (similar to the Spanish colonial practices), or if it should pursue a decentralized political model reflecting the distribution of power in the evolving, revolutionary American model (and in Spain shortly before independence). In theory, the Liberals favored the American and Spanish liberal model. The Liberals, led by Benito Juárez, eventually permanently established themselves in power after the defeat of the French-Conservative alliance in 1867. Juárez, according to many critics, failed to strengthen the legislative and judicial branches. Instead, he legitimized the practice of continuing in office, an issue contributing significantly to the cause of the Mexican Revolution of 1910. When Porfirio Díaz replaced Juárez's successor through a rebellion, he too followed his former mentor and ensconced himself in power through seven undemocratic reelections. The revolution had been fought on the political principles of effective suffrage and no-reelection. However, General Álvaro Obregón, president from 1920–24, following in the footsteps of Juárez and Díaz, changed the Constitution of 1917, incorporating numerous Liberal principles, and won the presidential election of 1928. He was assassinated before taking office. Revolutionary leaders led by General Plutarco Elías Calles revoked a constitutional amendment allowing reelection and created a national party whose members would control the political system for the next seven decades.

The second major political theme separating Liberals from Conservatives was the Liberal view that the Catholic Church's social, economic and political role was an impediment to Mexico's development politically and economically. Its views toward the Church were incorporated into the Constitution of 1857. Severe constitutional restrictions placed on the Church were not enforced during the latter years of the Porfiriato, but the revolutionaries, many of whom were products of hundreds of Liberal clubs in the 1900s desirous of reviving basic Liberal principles from the nineteenth century, incorporated equally harsh restrictions in the 1917 Constitution. They limited the Church's educational role, its economic influence, and its impact on politics. Some of these restrictions were eliminated in 1992 reforms to the Constitution while others still remain in effect today.

Who started the Mexican-American War and how did it affect relations with the United States?

Historians are in agreement that the United States government, led by President James K. Polk, provoked Mexico into a war to protect its national territory from American intervention. Polk had blatant territorial ambitions, and in 1845 the U.S. Congress approved the annexation of the independent Republic of Texas, which Mexico still considered to be part of its national territory. Polk was not satisfied with Texas alone and wanted to buy part of New Mexico and California. The Mexicans refused his offer, and Mexican and U.S. forces clashed briefly. Congress then declared war on Mexico on May 13, 1846. The United States invaded Mexican territory in New Mexico, California, and Texas, and occupied the port of Veracruz. General Winfield Scott led troops from Veracruz to Mexico City, taking the capital after a bitter fight in March 1847. Mexico's resistance to the U.S. invasion is best symbolized by the deaths of six military cadets, known as *Los Niños Heroes* (The Child Heroes), who jumped off Chapultepec Castle rather than surrender. The United States used its occupation to force the 1848 Treaty of Guadalupe Hidalgo on Mexico, in which Mexico lost 55 percent of its national territory, including all or parts of Nevada, Colorado, Utah, California, Arizona, New Mexico, and Texas, in exchange for $15 million.

The United States' aggression toward Mexico further increased Mexicans' sense of nationalism, and particularly as directed toward the United States, elements of which exist to date. These historic events led to Mexico's distrust of the United States. This distrust has not only been reflected in the public posture of Mexico toward the United States in its bilateral relationship with its northern neighbor, but also can be found even in concrete policy decisions. Until the 1990s, the stated national security mission of the Mexican armed forces was to defend Mexico at all costs from an American invasion. The Mexican Army's unwillingness to collaborate significantly with the U.S. military is a consequence, in part, of this historic event. Mexico also passed laws after the Mexican Revolution preventing foreigners (but largely directed at Americans specifically) from owning any property within a certain distance of its borders, as well as direct, legal ownership of real estate anywhere. These restrictions on property ownership again can be traced back to the Mexican-American War, and the way in which Polk and the Democratic Party used the Texas Republic (to which Mexico had allowed heavy immigration by American settlers) to establish a foothold by the United States in its northern territories.

Who was Benito Juárez?

Sometimes referred to as "Mexico's Lincoln," Benito Juárez was the most important figure in the first two-thirds of the nineteenth century and the political father of Mexican liberalism. Benito Juárez was born in the poor southern state of Oaxaca in 1806. He was able to attend law school in Oaxaca, graduating in 1834, despite the fact that he came from humble Zapotec indigenous origins. He became a practicing lawyer and a local political leader and judge. But Conservative forces dissolved the state legislature while Juárez was serving in it. During the 1840s, the Liberals clashed violently with the Conservatives, the leading opposing political party. Juárez became governor of his home state, as a Liberal Party member, in 1847. Eventually, the Liberals defeated the Conservatives, and Juárez was appointed president of the Supreme Court in 1857, a post which made him next in line for the presidency. Shortly thereafter, the Conservatives staged a coup, and Juárez succeeded to the presidency constitutionally, leading to a civil war from 1858 to 1861 known as the War of the Reform.

During the civil conflict, the Liberals, under Juárez's leadership, issued radical reform laws that severely attacked the Catholic Church's economic and social influence, and restricted the Church's ability to acquire revenues and perpetuate its economic influence through its control over real property. The Liberals again succeeded in defeating the Conservatives by 1861, and in March, Juárez was re-elected president. When his government suspended payments of its foreign debt, the French used it as an excuse to intervene and establish an empire in collaboration with the Conservatives from 1862 to 1867, imposing Archduke Maximilian on the throne. Juárez led the Liberal forces against the French and Conservatives, ultimately defeating them after years of warfare. Juárez ran for the presidency in 1867, which many of his Liberal colleagues opposed, raising the issue of no reelection. In 1871, he again ran for the presidency, but Congress decided the election, granting him the office. He died in 1872. Strongly criticized during his lifetime for his multiple reelections to the presidency and for his strengthening of presidential power, he nevertheless remained a major symbol of Mexican nationalism for his leadership against the French.

What was the War of the Reform?

In the 1830s, Liberals and Conservatives began an ideological battle for control of Mexico's political future. These ideological conflicts led to constant fighting between the forces supporting both movements. The Liberals favored a decentralized, federalist form of government, restrictions on the social and economic influence of the Catholic Church, and economic support of small landholders. The Conservatives favored a strong, central government dominated by the executive branch, a fundamental role for the Church, indeed an alliance between church and state, and support for large manufacturing firms. The War of the Reform, sometimes referred to as the Three Years War, took place from 1858 to 1861. It resulted from a Conservative reaction to the radical Liberal laws passed during the 1855–57 government of Juan N. Alvarez and Ignacio Comonfort. Historians typically refer to three notable pieces of Liberal legislation named after the cabinet ministers responsible for initiating their respective new laws or *leyes*. The Ley Lerdo directly attacked the economic basis of the Catholic Church by forcing corporate owners, such as the Church, to sell their huge landholdings. It was passed in the hope of depriving the Church of its wealth and stimulating economic growth by making millions of acres available to the public. Unfortunately, they also applied the law to the collective holdings of indigenous communities, leading to exploitation of the indigenous communities and a loss of tribal property. The Ley Juárez, named after Benito Juárez, eliminated and restricted special legal rights that the military and the Church had retained from the colonial era. Finally, the Ley Iglesias introduced legislation that limited the Church's ability to charge high fees for performing Catholic sacraments, another important source of Church income.

These three laws and other equally radical Liberal legislation were incorporated into the 1857 Constitution. The government secularized cemeteries, removing Church control and an additional source of income. Once again, both sides gathered their forces, each controlling different geographic sections of Mexico, with the Conservatives fighting against the implementation of these laws from 1858 to 1861, and repealing them in those regions they controlled. The Liberals finally achieved political and military supremacy in 1861, defeating the Conservative armies. Juárez became president in March 1861, setting the stage for the French intervention and an alliance between the Conservatives, the Church, and the French.

Why was the Constitution of 1857 so important?

The 1857 Constitution remained in effect from 1857 to 1917, making it the most durable national legal document after that of the current 1917 Constitution. A careful reading of the 1857 Constitution clearly reflects the important political and social principles of nineteenth-century Mexico as interpreted by the Liberal Party (which eventually defeated its Conservative opponents after a series of civil wars). The 1857 constitution exerted a significant impact on Mexico's political history in the late 1850s and the 1860s, after the Liberals incorporated its most radical legislation directed against the Catholic Church into the actual Constitution. By giving national, symbolic legitimacy to the radical anti-Church beliefs, it provoked Conservatives to resist the Liberals more strongly in the ensuing War of the Reform, 1858–61. Furthermore, in their desperation to defeat the Liberals and restore themselves and the Church and military allies to power, the Conservatives formed an ultimately disastrous alliance with the French and imposed a monarch on Mexico, a decision having important implications for Mexican nationalism and the principle of nonintervention.

The principles established in the Constitution of the United Mexican States influenced the Mexican Revolution of 1910 and the subsequent political issues that characterized the country after the approval of the 1917 Constitution. The most important principles included in the constitution were those that described the rights and structures of a federal system, sharing many similarities with the U.S. Constitution, including freedom of speech, freedom of press, the division of powers into three branches of government, the right to bear arms, and municipal autonomy, as well uniquely Mexican provisions such as the limitation on the Church to own real property and the elimination of special courts and privileges for the military and the Church.

During the administration of Porfirio Díaz, many of these political principles were ignored and abused, but the Constitution was not amended or replaced. At the turn of the century many Mexicans, opposed to the authoritarian behavior of the Díaz regime, wanted to restore in practice the basic Liberal principles found in the Constitution. They established numerous local Liberal clubs that brought together like-minded opponents of the regime. Many of these individuals became active in the revolt against Díaz, and contributed significantly to political leadership during and after the revolution. The 1917 Constitution reaffirmed many of the basic political principles, restoring the original Liberal political values, while at the same time it incorporated social and economic principles (such as severe restrictions on the Catholic Church) that were far more radical than those found in the 1857 document.

Who was Porfirio Díaz and what was the Porfiriato?

Porfirio Díaz, who came from the Mexican state of Oaxaca, was born in 1830 and studied law under Benito Juárez. He left his legal studies to join the army during the Mexican-American War. Eventually he became a war hero and one of the most influential generals in the Liberal army, fighting against the Conservatives and the French intervention in the 1850s and 1860s. After the Liberals defeated the French and Conservative alliance in 1867, and his mentor Juárez became president, Díaz led a rebellion in opposition to Juárez's reelection in 1871, but he was defeated in 1872. In 1876, he led another rebellion, known as the Plan de Tuxtepec, against Juárez's successor, President Sebastian Lerdo de Tejada. He eventually defeated government forces and formally became president in 1877, but relinquished the presidency to another Liberal general, Manuel González, in 1881. He returned to the presidency in 1884 and remained in office until May 25, 1911. The formative years at the end of the nineteenth century, from 1884–1911, became known as the Porfiriato, that is, the period dominated by Porfirio Díaz.

The Porfiriato is identified with numerous characteristics, politically, economically, and socially. The most important political characteristic of Díaz's long reign is his personal control and continuity in office. Similar to some of the long-reigning viceroys of the colonial period, Diaz acquired significant political power and authority, using this authority increasingly to dominate political decision-making. He was a skilled politician, able to consolidate his power through many

techniques, including playing off political and military competitors against one another. Moreover, he selected most of
the candidates for the Mexican Congress, sometimes running
the same individual for more than one district and state.
Given his long reign, Díaz's presence became synonymous
with the stability of the political system itself.

Díaz introduced or facilitated important economic changes
in the development of Mexico during this era. Among the
most important characteristics of his regime was the introduction of foreign investment and foreign control over
numerous sectors of the economy. He gave out generous concessions to foreigners to develop Mexican railroads. He also
believed that attracting immigrants from Europe and the
United States would help develop Mexico's vast agricultural
resources, offering such individuals cheap prices for large
tracts of land. Instead of producing the kind of influx of
farmer-settlers who came to the United States in the nineteenth
century, Mexico attracted wealthy investors who bought huge
tracts of land, complementing those large holdings already
held by influential Mexican families.

Socially, the Porfiriato became noted for enhancing social
inequalities and particularly for the exploitation and repression
of the indigenous populations. For example, some of his wealthy
political allies sought to gain control of fertile lands in northwestern Mexico controlled by the Yaqui Indians. When the
Yaquis resisted, they were brutally suppressed, and hundreds
were killed and hung from telegraph poles as a lesson to their
peers. Their families were broken up, and many were shipped
to Yucatán as forced labor on the henequen plantations, where
they died in large numbers from abuse and disease.

What were the long-term consequences of the Porfiriato for the 20th century?

The Porfiriato, the period encompassing Porfirio Díaz's long
reign over Mexican politics, 1884–1911, produced numerous

long-term consequences for Mexico's development politically, economically, and socially, into the twentieth century. Politically, the most long-lasting impact of the Porfiriato on Mexico's evolution was the rejection of personalistic, authoritarian, and continuous leadership, which took many decades to evolve after Díaz was overthrown in 1911 by the Revolution. The most significant political motto of the revolutionaries was "Effective Suffrage and No-Reelection," in reaction to Díaz imposing himself for decades, but it took nearly another century to actually implement the effective suffrage component of that principle. After 1920, when regular elections once again became the norm, General Álvaro Obregón did modify the no-reelection principle by amending the 1917 Constitution. Obregón was actually reelected after skipping a term, but he was assassinated before taking office. His assassination ended forever any alteration in the no reelection principle, which became an underlying principle of contemporary Mexican politics. It was misinterpreted and applied as well to the legislative branch in 1934, although qualified by the word "consecutive." This change in the legislative electoral process produced significant consequences by weakening the legislative branch versus the executive branch. It also made legislators dependent on party members from the executive branch for nominations for decades. To this day, the government has been unable to repeal the no consecutive reelection principle in the legislative branch. Most analysts consider this principle to be a serious impediment to the balance of power between the branches of government. Nevertheless, after 1920, the postrevolutionary elite succeeded in creating a party that enabled them to maintain control over the presidency.

Economically and socially, the failures and prejudices of the Porfiriato resulted in some unique principles being incorporated in the 1917 Constitution. The Constitution legitimized a mixed economic model of state capitalism. The state took on a larger role after 1920, ostensibly to protect and increase economic benefits for working-class Mexicans. The actual benefits were limited, even though organized labor became a major political supporter of the postrevolutionary party and its leaders. The state placed subsoil resources, such as valuable minerals and oil, in the hands of the nation, to be administered by the state, so all Mexicans would become economic beneficiaries. This principle was a response to the wealthy concessionaries who received valuable property at bargain prices from the Díaz administration. Socially, the racial prejudices encouraged by the Porfiriato also generated a reaction in favor of promoting policies that highlighted the dignity of the individual and greater social equality. For example, the government hoped to provide free, public education to all Mexicans through elementary school. Under the leadership of several notable secretaries of public education in the 1920s and 1930s, efforts were made to implement these constitutional and intellectual goals, but the government fell far short of actually fulfilling these principles, many of which were put in place in reaction to the Porfiriato's failures.

8

THE MEXICAN REVOLUTION AND A NEW POLITICAL MODEL FOR MEXICO

THE MEXICAN REVOLUTION

What were the causes of the Mexican Revolution of 1910?

Historians have argued for a century about which were the most important causes of the Mexican Revolution. Although each historian ranks different causes as more or less important, there is little disagreement about what explanations should be on everyone's list. The importance of those explanations varies according to the geographic region being examined and the social class background of the individual participant. Regardless of the reason given, the most important of these causes are represented in the fundamental articles of the 1917 Constitution. Many of the Mexicans who lived in northern Mexico and participated in the revolution did so due to their experiences with foreigners who owned mines, large properties, and railroads. Working-class Mexicans who were employed in foreign-owned companies typically viewed themselves as second-class citizens. For example, in the railroads they were not given the skilled, engineering positions, but instead were assigned to the unskilled positions. One of the goals of mining engineers graduating from the National School of Engineering as late as the 1940s was to occupy all of the professional engineering positions in every foreign-owned mine in Mexico. This antiforeign sentiment is reflected in the fact that the Constitution assigned subsoil rights to the nation, rather than viewing them as private property.

A second fundamental cause of the revolution, from the point of view of working Mexicans, was labor rights. During the Porfiriato from 1884 to 1911, strikes were not permitted. The Díaz administration was renowned for suppressing labor strikes, particularly during the last decade of his administration. Two such occurrences include the Cananea Mining demonstration in Sonora in 1906, where Arizona Rangers crossed the border as strikebreakers, and the notorious Río Blanco Mill strike in Puebla in 1909, where dozens of workers lost their lives. These and other labor activities and strikes led to numerous demands for improved working conditions for all Mexicans, including maximum hours per day, minimum percentages of Mexican workers in foreign-owned plants, and minimum wages. The most important principle, which became Article 123 of the Constitution, was granting labor the right to strike. For rural workers, both mestizo and indigenous, who were typically even more exploited than their urban counterparts, the revolution meant land for peasants who wanted their own farms. Land was a central issue for the men and women who supported Emiliano Zapata, a leader who emerged from Morelos. Such abuses as debt servitude and the use of company stores (stores owned by the landowner) were also prohibited in the revolutionary articles incorporated in the Constitution.

Additionally, middle-class Mexicans, professional people, and intellectuals were strongly interested in political change, either because they desired a democratic polity ideologically or because they harbored political ambitions themselves and were hopeful for more upward political mobility as a consequence of civil violence. The most important political principles, advocated strongly by Francisco I. Madero, who had opposed Díaz in the 1910 presidential election, were effective suffrage and no reelection. The phrase "Effective

Suffrage and No Reelection," appeared at the bottom of every official correspondence from the federal government until well into the 1970s, indicative of its symbolic importance to the post-revolutionary leadership. Many politicized Mexicans also wanted municipal autonomy, having experienced the intervention of authoritarian state or federal entities.

Who was Francisco I. Madero?

Francisco Madero, born in 1873, was a wealthy landowner from Coahuila, a northern border state below Texas. The son of a prominent industrialist and businessman, he and many of his relatives opposed Díaz's authoritarian regime. Madero was not a radical revolutionary, but an individual with a social conscience who wanted to change how Mexico was led politically and the direction it pursued socially. He treated his own employees humanely, providing them with health benefits, access to schools for their children, and an adequate salary. In 1905, he began his anti-reelectionist activities and founded the Benito Juárez Anti-reelectionist Club to oppose Porfirio Díaz's continued reelection as president. In 1908, he published an influential book titled *The Presidential Succession of 1910*, in which he laid out some of his basic principles and criticized the president for his antidemocratic practices. That same year, President Díaz, in an interview with an American journalist, made the statement that the 1910 election would be democratic, opening the door for an opposition candidate. Madero took him at his word and eventually became the candidate of the Anti-Reelectionist Party, running on the motto of "Effective Suffrage and No Reelection." He conducted a national campaign, but in the final stages, he was arrested and imprisoned in San Luis Potosí. Díaz declared himself the winner in a fraudulent election. Madero was able to leave Mexico and go to San Antonio, Texas, where he issued his famous Plan of San Luis Potosi, which contains many of his prominent principles.

Madero ultimately crossed back into Mexico in 1911 and led a revolution in the northern states. Using a victory over the federal army in Ciudad Juárez led by Pancho Villa and Pascual Orozco as leverage, he forced Díaz and his vice president to resign in May 1911. Madero did not seize the presidency; instead he allowed an interim president, while he ran for and won the presidency in a new election in late 1911, taking office in November. Madero and his vice president, José María Pino Suárez, governed for two years, during which time he faced considerable opposition from former supporters of Díaz, as well as from more radical revolutionaries such as Emiliano Zapata, who were interested in land reform and other socially radical policies. Madero did not provide the strong leadership necessary to weaken his political enemies, who instead, led by General Victoriano Huerta, a career federal officer under Díaz, overthrew Madero and murdered both him and his vice president on February 18, 1913. Madero's murder provided the catalyst for the truly violent and radical phase of the Mexican Revolution, from 1913 to 1916. This period determined the major revolutionary principles found in the 1917 Constitution and the violence until 1920 and beyond. The U.S. ambassador's complicity in allowing Madero to be overthrown and murdered also contributed significantly to Mexicans' nationalistic views of and distrust toward the United States.

Who really was Pancho Villa?

Born (José) Doroteo Arango (Arámbula) in 1878, Pancho (Francisco) Villa was the son of poor peasants who worked on one of the largest landholdings in the state of Durango. He helped support his brothers and sister when his father died, eventually becoming a member of a bandit gang, after which he left the state in 1902 and settled in Chihuahua. He continued his illegal activities and joined Pascual Orozco, with other riders that he recruited, in a revolt against Díaz in 1911. Villa participated in the victorious attack on Ciudad Juárez, which gave Madero a decisive victory over federal troops and the ability to force Díaz to resign. President Madero saved Villa from a firing squad, after which Villa escaped from prison. When General Victoriano Huerta led a military coup against Madero and had him murdered in 1913, he also killed Abraham González, a friend of Villa's, who originally recruited Villa to Madero's cause in 1910. Villa gathered up a force of supporters and declared his support for the Constitutionalist Army led by Venustiano Carranza. This army was composed of Mexicans who wanted to restore constitutional government and defeat the reactionary forces aligned with Huerta. Briefly provisional governor of Chihuahua in 1913–14, Villa implemented radical policies in seizing property from large landholders and converting numerous privately owned buildings into schools.

Villa was very popular in Chihuahua and was able to recruit large numbers of men to join his army. He seized cattle and traded it for arms across the border in the United States. He became one of the most effective generals in the Constitutionalist Army of the North. Villa commandeered trains to carry his cavalry. He used the railroad system effectively to create a highly mobile force. In 1914, he defeated the federal army in the Battle of Zacatecas, a decisive victory in ousting Huerta. The victorious generals joined together in the Convention of Aguascalientes, proposing some radical solutions to Mexico's economic and social problems, but their views were opposed by Carranza. Villa, Emiliano Zapata, and others chose to oppose Carranza and his allies, most notably General Álvaro Obregón, which initiated another phase of the civil war from 1914–1916. Villa and his army were ultimately defeated by Obregón in the Battle of Celaya, 1915, with Obregón using modern battle techniques developed for World War I to destroy Villa's cavalry charges. Villa, who lost the support of the United States and was deprived of access to additional weapons, sent his troops across the border to attack the U.S. cavalry garrison at Columbus, New Mexico, on March 9, 1916. This attack led to the Pershing Expedition, headed by General John "Black Jack" Pershing, who unsuccessfully pursued Villa's forces in northern Mexico. Unable to defeat Carranza's troops, Villa eventually settled for a large ranch from the government for his men and their families, but was assassinated in 1923, with the complicity of government officials. Today, he remains a major figure in Mexican popular culture.

Who benefited most from the Mexican Revolution?

Historians have never fully agreed whether or not Mexico underwent a truly social revolution. Regardless of the depth or definition of its revolution, the cost in human lives and property destruction was devastating. Mexico, similar to most countries which have undergone significant revolutions, went through multiple phases between 1910 and 1920. The incumbent regime was easily eliminated without much bloodshed by 1911, but the initial, moderate victors who governed from 1911 to 1913 were removed violently by a counterrevolution. That counterrevolution produced the first truly violent phase of the revolution, won by the revolutionaries in 1914. But the revolutionaries themselves, again similar to those found in other historic revolutions, including that of the Soviet Union, had a falling out over the path the revolution should take. Essentially, those favoring more radical solutions to the maldistribution of land and other social and economic ills were defeated by those revolutionaries who favored more modest reforms. The moderates, under Venustiano Carranza, took control of the government in 1916. But at the end of the decade, General Álvaro Obregón, Carranza's leading general in defeating the more radical revolutionary forces, wanted to pursue more socially reformist policies, placing himself ideologically somewhere between Carranza and the revolutionaries he himself had defeated in 1914–15.

An examination of the beneficiaries of the Mexican Revolution makes clear that those most favored politically were members of the rising middle class. Generally speaking, these individuals, who held political posts after 1920, were members of an educated, professional class, most of whom had not actively participated in the revolution. The most adversely affected individuals were Mexicans from wealthy entrepreneurial and landholding families, whose representation in the political class was nearly eliminated altogether. Those Mexicans who had fought in the revolution, typically coming from modest, working-class rural families, dominated leadership during the revolutionary years, especially from 1914 to 1920, but not during the institutionalized post-revolutionary period. Except for the revolutionary generals who became presidents for most of the period from 1920 to 1946, the majority of national figures were civilians. It took numerous decades after 1920 before the standard of living of large groups of poorer Mexicans improved. This improvement occurred typically during the 1950s and 1960s, which witnessed the largest increase in the size of the middle class and the longest era of economic growth, and therefore resulted in a concomitant decrease in the percentage of Mexicans falling into the working class.

Could Mexico have achieved changes in its structures through peaceful means instead of violence?

Historians and citizens alike, when evaluating the consequences of civil wars and violent revolutions, often wonder in retrospect if structural change could have occurred through peaceful rather than violent means, avoiding the great loss of life and the accompanying physical destruction. To what extent did Mexico alter its political and economic structures after 1920? Politically, it is possible to measure some significant changes in the composition and patterns of leadership that were brought about by the revolution. For example, recent research empirically demonstrates that for a brief period of time, especially in the 1920s and 1930s, ambitious Mexicans from modest, working-class backgrounds, and from small provincial communities and villages, gained access to national political office and state governorships. Such Mexicans in leadership positions never came close to representing the percentage of all Mexicans from these socioeconomic circumstances; nevertheless they represented the highest percentage of such Mexicans to achieve important political office before or since.

One of the important credentials, and therefore structures important to upward political mobility before the revolution, was a college degree. Certain public universities and preparatory schools were particularly important in producing future political leaders. Mexico achieved a remarkably high level of college-educated politicians prior to 1911. After 1920, college degrees were not valued to the same degree as before the revolution, and it took decades before prominent political figures achieved educational levels equal to their pre-revolutionary peers.

It is more difficult to measure the structural economic changes wrought by the revolution. Many historians are not in agreement that Mexico underwent a "true" social revolution because they do not find adequate evidence of such major economic changes. The most universal of such economic alterations could be reflected in land ownership. There is no question that the Mexican government, depending on the specific presidential administration, began to distribute land as early as 1915 to landless peasants. Eventually, the largest amounts of land were distributed to farmers through the ejido system, a land tenure system based on the indigenous principle of assigning land to villages collectively. To each resident who wanted to farm, this system granted rights to use the land and to pass the land on to their children, but not to pass on an actual deed to the land. The government continued to give out lands for most of the twentieth century, breaking up most of the large landholdings in Mexico. While millions of peasants obtained their own land, the government never provided adequate credit to make these farms productive, nor in many cases adequate amounts of land on which to make a living. Peasants could not borrow from private banks because they did not own the land. By the 1960s, most of the ejido properties were being illegally rented and consolidated into larger farms. Thus, the argument can be made that the revolution produced a more equitable redistribution of land, but at the same time did little to improve the concrete economic welfare of the recipients.

How did the revolution alter political institutions and civil-military relations?

If we examine the political development and institutional relationships following the revolution in the 1920s and 1930s, it becomes clear that the foundations for the political relationships that characterized Mexico for the next century can be traced to that period. It is essential to note that the Mexicans who succeeded in taking control of the political process after 1920, with few exceptions, were part of the revolutionary forces that determined the outcome of the decade of violence from 1910 to 1920. The senior generals became the presidents, the secretaries of national defense, the provincial zone commanders, and often the governors during the next two decades. Because these generals were the product of a popular army, in effect multiple guerrilla movements, they had to institutionalize the officer corps and to gradually eliminate large numbers of veterans from active duty. The leadership established a new military school, which became the Heroic Military College, in the 1920s. It developed an authoritarian and strict curriculum focused on obedience to one's superior officer and to the president. This was a remarkable achievement because declining portions of the existing popular army revolted, without success, against the government in 1923, 1927, and 1929.

The revolutionary generals, under the leadership of ex-president Plutarco Elías Calles and after the assassination of president-elect Álvaro Obregón in 1928, decided to create a political organization, the National Revolutionary Party, to co-opt politically ambitious individuals, military and civilian alike, and create a substitute for personalistic leadership. It is clear that while Calles initiated this concept to further his own personal political ambitions, he unintentionally provided a structure for a circulating, collective elite that emerged from the revolutionary era. President Lázaro Cardenas, one of the last revolutionary generals to govern Mexico, added several additional features that strengthened the control of civilian actors, while concentrating more influence in the executive branch. He formalized four sectors in the party, creating a corporatist system in which occupational groups would be represented in the party organization and in congress. He established unions and business organizations to channel those groups' demands to the government. To strengthen his own position as president and eliminate his subordination to his former mentor, General Calles, Cárdenas altered the Constitution to prevent members of the lower chamber of congress from being consecutively reelected. This weakened congress while strengthening executive power over the nominees for congressional seats. Although numerous other political principles emerged from the revolutionary era, the principles of military subordination to civilian control and a strong, unified political organization controlled by a dominant executive branch determined many aspects of the political process until 2000.

What was the attitude of the United States toward the revolution?

The United States had maintained good relations with Porfirio Díaz prior to the opening days of the revolution in 1910. In fact, an examination of the activities of the U.S. government on behalf of Mexico in the decade immediately preceding the revolution are indicative of a collaborative relationship between the two countries. The United States helped the Díaz government persecute some of the more radical anti-Díaz figures in the labor movement, the most notable example of which were the Flores Magón brothers, who were significant precursors of the revolution. Ricardo and Enrique Flores Magón were forced into exile in San Antonio, Texas, where they were able to publish their anti-regime newspaper, *Regeneración*, one of the most influential publications in converting Mexicans to the revolutionary cause. They were forced to move to St. Louis, which hosted a large exile community of pro-revolutionaries, but, as was the case in San Antonio, they were harassed by police, and some supporters were imprisoned. Ricardo was arrested in 1907, and tried and imprisoned in Arizona from 1909 to 1910. Other revolutionaries fared better. Pancho Villa, for example, cultivated contacts along the Texas border, including U.S. Army commanders. Authorities winked at his exchange of cattle for weapons during the early years of the revolution.

When Francisco Madero became president, Henry Lane Wilson, the American ambassador, interfered repeatedly in Mexican affairs, attempting to undercut the president's legitimacy. Most tragically, he colluded with General Victoriano Huerta to remove Madero by force, ultimately leading to the murder of the president and the vice president by the usurpers. President Woodrow Wilson came to office in 1914 and resisted Ambassador Wilson's recommendation to recognize the Huerta regime. He removed Wilson and decided to provide aid to the Constitutionalist Army opposing the Huerta regime. But using an incident involving the U.S. Navy in the port of Veracruz, President Wilson ordered the occupation of the port by U.S. forces. Mexicans from all over the republic responded to this blatant intervention, organizing groups of volunteers, including students, to travel to Veracruz to oppose the Americans.

When Huerta was finally ousted by Constitutionalists and the victorious revolutionaries embarked on another violent phase of the revolution, the United States intervened once again. This time it chased Villa's troops after they crossed the border and attacked Columbus, New Mexico, in March 1916. Ultimately, the U.S. government chose to recognize Venustiano Carranza's administration. Regardless of its motivations or the individual factions it supported from 1911 to 1920, the United States pursued an actively interventionist agenda in Mexico, including a range of strategies from the use of force to financial support.

What is the Constitution of 1917?

In order to understand Mexico's development throughout most of the twentieth century and many of its current policies, it is essential to understand the most important articles of the 1917 Constitution. The 1917 Constitution, currently in effect, emerged from the violent confrontations during the revolutionary decade, especially from those events occurring during 1911–16. Mexico held a special constitutional convention, electing representatives from every state. Many of these individuals advocated an ideological posture reflecting the major social, economic, and political goals of the revolution, a posture that was far more radical than the beliefs subscribed to by the 1916–20 government of Venustiano Carranza. The 1917 Constitution became an essential component of the rhetoric of the Mexican Revolution, legitimizing numerous concepts for the Mexican public, who developed a reverence for its basic principles.

It can be argued that one of the principles that emerged from the revolutionary era represented symbolically by this document is constitutionalism. Expressed differently, the fundamental principles contained in the constitution have achieved a legitimacy in the eyes of most Mexicans that exceeds their legal status. The influence of constitutionalism in the popular culture can be illustrated by the fact that in various cities in Mexico, including the national capital, streets are named after the most important individual articles, not just the word Constitution, a common practice in older American towns and villages. For example, in Tijuana, there is an arch known as Calle Articulo 123, which is located near Revolución and First Street, not far from Constitución. Articles 3, 27, and 130 also are the names of important streets in major cities and state capitals.

If one had to summarize the most important principles found in these four articles, you could refer to the most significant causes of the Mexican Revolution. Article 3, which is devoted to education, requires that government ensure that education at the elementary, secondary, and normal levels is free of religious influence; that elementary education is compulsory and free; and that it promotes the dignity of the individual and equal rights. Article 27 focuses on ownership of land and water, and the need to divide up large landed estates to develop small landholdings. It states that ownership of all natural resources shall belong to the nation, which shall grant concessions to exploit those resources. This article also banned, until the 1992 reforms, the ownership of any real property by religious institutions. Foreigners were not allowed to acquire direct ownership of lands or waters within one hundred kilometers of the borders or fifty kilometers along the shores. Article 123 established labor rights, including a maximum limit of eight hours of work a day, the right of workers to organize, the right to strike, and, most interestingly, the enactment of a social security law. Article 130 detailed numerous restrictions on churches, including no legal standing for religious groups, the freedom of religion, marriage as a civil contract, that ministers be Mexican by birth, that churches obtain government permission to build new places of worship, that ministers may not inherit real property, and that ministers may never publicly or in privately organized groups criticize the laws of the nation or the government.

What was the cultural impact of the Mexican Revolution on painting, music, and literature?

The Mexican Revolution of 1910 influenced many aspects of Mexico's development, but less is known of the tremendous impact it exerted on culture in and outside of Mexico. The social aspects of the revolutionary ideology influenced the content, methodology, and philosophy of art, music, and literature. Of the three cultural categories, the artistic impact was most wide ranging. A generation of artists, including Diego Rivera, José Clemente Orozco, and David Alfaro Siqueiros believed that painting should be a medium accessible to all Mexicans, regardless of their social class. By painting only on canvas, they argued that art would be restricted to a small group of Mexicans who could afford to buy it and keep it in their homes and offices. Their view was also shared by José Vasconcelos, the first minister of public education in the 1920s, who used public funding to support artists and encourage them to paint on the walls of public buildings, using the fresco (wet plaster) technique. These projects often involved large physical spaces and therefore incorporated the contributions of other artists and assistants, supporting another philosophical concept that art could be a collaborative venture. But many of these artists also wanted to use their art to convey a social or political message, ranging from a view that the Spanish exploited and abused the indigenous population during the colonization of New Spain to the corruption of politicians and the entrepreneurial class in the 1930s and 1940s.

In literature, Mexican authors such as Mariano Azuela used the novel to identify many themes of the revolution and the failures of the post-revolutionary regimes. His novel *The Underdogs*, for example, became the most widely read fictional work in the public school system, influencing the views of generations of Mexican adults. Other contemporaries also took up important indigenous themes, presenting the native cultures in a much more favorable light. The vibrancy of all of the cultural activity in Mexico during the post-revolutionary era was viewed abroad as a creative and supportive environment for foreign artists, photographers, novelists, and crafts persons, including D. H. Lawrence, who spent two years in Mexico and authored *The Plumed Serpent* about indigenous culture, and Katherine Anne Porter, who worked in Mexico from 1918 to 1921, wrote a number of stories set in Mexico, and publicized the ongoing cultural changes in a nonfiction *Outline of Mexican Popular Arts and Crafts* in 1922. The revolution also stimulated the incorporation of cultural themes organic to Mexico, even affecting classical music, represented in *Sinfonia India,* the widely performed work of composer Carlos Chávez, who used his leadership of Mexico's National Conservatory of Music, Mexico's Symphonic Orchestra, and the National Institute of Fine Arts to promote indigenous themes in musical compositions and performances, and in other mediums. These indigenous themes also have become well known outside of the country through the international performances of the Ballet Foklórico de México since 1952.

THE EVOLUTION OF MODERN POLITICAL STRUCTURES AFTER 1920

Why did the assassination of President-elect Álvaro Obregón alter Mexico's political future?

General Álvaro Obregón was president of Mexico from 1920 to 1924 and the first figure to complete a presidential term after the implementation of the 1917 Constitution. His administration was followed by that of Plutarco Elías Calles, another northern revolutionary general, who completed his term between 1924 and 1928. One of the central provisions of the Constitution responding to Porfirio Díaz's blatant abuse in maintaining himself in office for seven consecutive periods was a prohibition, in Article 83, against serving as president more than one time, regardless of being elected or appointed previously. Obregón, politically ambitious and desirous of becoming president a second time, persuaded his supporters in Congress to amend the Constitution to permit nonconsecutive reelection, allowing him to run for the presidency in 1928. Many army officers, civilians, and students were strongly opposed to his running for reelection, and some were murdered by government forces in 1927. Nevertheless, Obregón won the election; but shortly thereafter, before taking office, he was assassinated by a Catholic fanatic. His unexpected death set in motion a series of crucial political changes.

Because Mexico does not have a vice president, the Constitution provides a process whereby the Congress chooses a temporary president and then holds a new election. Anticipating the new election in 1929, and wanting to create stability in the post-revolutionary leadership, General Calles and other prominent military and civilian politicians established a national political party, the National Party of the Revolution (PNR), and ran a candidate for the presidency. Calles himself hoped to use the party to further his own ambitions, but he was unable to extend his influence beyond June 1935. This was when his former protégé, General Lázaro Cárdenas, who had won the 1934 election as the PNR's second presidential candidate, exiled his mentor to the United States. The PNR (later PRI) became the essential political vehicle for legitimizing presidential and government nominees for political office, winning every gubernatorial race until 1989, most senate and district congressional seats until the 1990s, and all presidential races until 2000. Popular opinion, strongly against presidential reelection, forced the Calles faction to reamend the Constitution in 1928 to reaffirm no-reelection. This has become inviolable in theory and in practice since 1929. Obregón's death set in motion two established principles of Mexican politics for most of the twentieth century. First, presidents could become powerful, personalist decision-makers, but only for the length of their terms. Second, self-perpetuating personal leaders like Díaz were replaced by a perpetual political organization (later named the PRI) allowing a rotating pool of ambitious politicians to govern Mexico for seven decades.

What was the influence of Plutarco Elías Calles on the formation of a modern Mexican state?

Plutarco Elías Calles formed part of a generation of self-made revolutionaries, who were born in the 1870s and supported the Constitutionalist Army during the revolution. From Sonora, he became involved during the initial phase of the revolution in support of Madero. Calles reached the rank of brigadier general by 1914, having joined the Constitutionalists in February 1913. He then served as the military commander and provisional governor of his home state from 1915 to 1917, and then as the constitutional governor, from 1917 to 1919. He did not become a senior general during the revolution, only reaching the rank of division general in 1920. He served as a cabinet member five times and twice as secretary of War, defeating antigovernment forces during an army rebellion in 1929. The political disciple of Álvaro Obregón, Calles ran for the presidency in 1923–24, becoming president in 1924 and serving a full term.

Calles made three notable contributions to the modern Mexican state, two while in the presidency and the third after leaving office. Historians correctly attribute many of the basic public financial institutions to the Calles presidency. Calles surrounded himself with capable individuals, including treasury secretary Alberto J. Pani and Manuel Gómez Morín, later the co-founder of the National Action Party. Gómez Morín was instrumental in devising important financial legislation, including that which established the Bank of Mexico, Mexico's equivalent of the U.S. Federal Reserve Bank. The creation of the bank and other credit institutions helped stabilize the economy and encourage economic growth.

In contrast to his institutional support for economic stability, Calles, an orthodox revolutionary who initially believed
in the radical articles incorporated into the Constitution of
1917, decided to implement severe restrictions on the Catholic
Church. The implementation of these laws led the Catholic
clergy to boycott holding masses and produced a popular
rebellion in many states among practicing Catholics, known
as the Cristero War (lasting from 1926 to 1929). Calles'
successor, Emilio Portes Gil, negotiated a secret agreement
with the Church to bring an end to the conflict, but the relationship between church and state remained strained for
decades. More important, these events reinforced state
superiority over the Church. The State nevertheless mod-
erated the application of some restrictions until definitive
reforms were enacted in the early 1990s, eliminating the most
offensive restrictions.

Finally, Álvaro Obregón won the presidential election as
Calles's successor in 1928, but was assassinated before taking
office, leaving Mexico in a highly vulnerable political situation.
Calles persuaded a top group of generals and civilian politicians to create a national party, the National Revolutionary
Party, to provide Mexico's political leadership and maintain
control over the political system, an institution which grew
into the dominant political organization, the PRI, for the rest
of the twentieth century.

What is the National Revolutionary Party (PNR)?

As the leading student of the establishment of the National
Revolutionary Party, Luis Javier Garrido, has noted, the PNR's
formation was largely the brainchild of President Plutarco
Elías Calles. Calles believed that a strong Mexican state could
not be created or survive without a national political organization that combined all military and civilian revolutionaries
under the umbrella of a central authority. Calles, leaving office
after the assassination of president-elect Obregón, recognized

the importance of creating such an organization to provide unity during the difficult political period that followed. He and his collaborators worked in 1928–29 to create the bylaws of the party, which brought together some 148 state and regional political organizations representing twenty-eight states and entities in Mexico. The party received financial support from the federal government, initially through monies withheld from federal bureaucrats' paychecks.

The party has gone through numerous structural changes, but the most important institutions established in the original 1929 statues, the National Executive Committee (CEN), the State Committees, and the Municipal Committees, remain intact. The National Executive Committee became the most influential decision-making body. In reality, between 1934 and the late 1990s, the president of the CEN was designated by the incumbent president, thus providing Mexico's chief executive a direct link to selecting candidates for national, state, and local offices, the most important of which were governors. Because the PNR was an amalgam of so many different parties and political factions, by definition the ideological composition of the party was broad and diverse.

What ultimately became the cornerstones of the party's structure were its corporatist pillars of support, composed of the most influential political and professional groups in Mexico. In the 1930s, the leadership of the National Executive Committee included an agrarian secretary and a labor secretary. These secretaries represented the two most populous groups of supporters led by the dominant labor unions of the day, the National Peasant Federation (CNC) and the Mexican Federation of Labor (CTM). In 1938, when the PNR changed its name to the Party of the Mexican Revolution (PRM), it added a third secretary to represent the "popular" sector. This sector included numerous professional organizations and white-collar workers who were gathered under a large confederation, similar to peasants and workers, known as the National Federation of Popular Organizations (CNOP).

Briefly, under the influence of President Cárdenas, the party added a fourth sector, the military, but it was short-lived, and President Manuel Avila Camacho (1940–46) removed it, suggesting instead that the military could be represented in the popular sector. These multiple organizations provided a huge base of support for the party through the following decades.

Who was Lázaro Cárdenas and how did he influence Mexico's political model?

Lázaro Cárdenas was born in a small community in Michoacán in 1895. He joined the revolution as a second captain in 1913 in support of the Constitutionalists. During the ensuing decade, he fought in numerous battles, including against the forces of Zapata and Villa, and served under his political mentor, General Plutarco Elías Calles. He also supported the government against army rebellions in 1923 and 1929, as well as against the Cristero Rebellion in 1928. He reached the rank of division general in 1928. He served as governor of his home state, president of the National Revolutionary Party (PNR), and secretary of National Defense, a position from which he resigned in 1934 to run as the PNR's candidate for president.

Calles apparently believed, when he influenced the decision to choose Cárdenas as the PNR's first official candidate for a full presidential term, that Cárdenas would acquiesce to Calles' leadership. In other words, Calles believed that he would be the power behind the throne. Cárdenas, unwilling to be subservient to Calles, used his political skills to outmaneuver the ex-president, forcefully exiling him to the United States in June 1935, less than seven months after taking office. In doing so, President Cárdenas introduced a major political principle of twentieth-century Mexican politics, that presidents would exercise control over the political system during, not after, their terms. Cárdenas' second major contribution to the Mexican political model was the development of some of the essential features of the National Revolutionary Party, as well as the corporatist structure between the state and various occupational groups. Cárdenas essentially created a formal relationship among organized labor and peasant organizations and his party, as well as most leading professional organizations. He recognized huge labor confederations as being incorporated into the party, and therefore having the stamp of approval from the state, creating a symbiotic relationship that lasted for decades. Furthermore, he tried to do the same with the private sector, requiring firms of a certain size to join state-initiated business organizations while excluding them from the party itself. Essentially, he created official channels of communication between the state and the most influential Mexican economic and political actors.

Finally, Cárdenas altered the social and economic tone of his administration to favor, at least rhetorically and sometimes in practice, the interests of the working classes, handing out land at a dramatically increased pace and encouraging greater numbers of legal strikes. On the other hand, by creating new political structures, including the corporatist linkages mentioned earlier, he established the basic foundation for a more powerful, centralized authoritarian state.

Why did Mexico nationalize the petroleum industry in 1939?

One of the underlying causes of the Revolution of 1910 was the degree of influence foreigners exercised in Mexico. (See question on causes of the Mexican Revolution.) During the Porfiriato from 1884–1911, numerous concessions were provided to foreign investors, ranging from the railroad right of ways to the exploitation of subsoil minerals, including petroleum, a resource with which Mexico was handsomely endowed. The victorious revolutionaries expressed a strong sense of nationalism that grew out of the revolutionary decade between 1910 and 1920 and was codified in the Constitution of 1917, including assigning all subsoil rights to the Mexican nation and requiring government approval to develop and exploit any mineral reserves. Another issue that emerged during the revolutionary decade and that explains the setting underlying the nationalization in 1939 was the importance of workers' rights, given the fact that they were not allowed to even strike prior to the revolution. The post-revolution presidents, beginning with Álvaro Obregón (1920–24), who relied on the support of organized labor to become president, encouraged labor's growth. By the 1930s, one of the economic sectors where labor-management conflicts became intense was the petroleum industry. Through the government labor arbitration board, Lázaro Cárdenas, who became president in 1934, legalized more strikes by labor during his administration than any of his predecessors.

All of the oil was being extracted by foreign companies from the United States and Europe. A recently formed labor union, whose demands for better pay and benefits were rejected by the oil companies, took its case to the Federal Conciliation and Arbitration Board, which ruled in favor of the union and allowed it to conduct a legal strike. The board issued a ruling against the companies, requiring them to pay millions in back wages. The companies refused to comply with the decision, taking their grievances to the Mexican Supreme Court, which ruled against their appeal. President Cárdenas, responding to the intractability of the firms, most of which refused to abide by the court's decision, decided he had no alternative but to expropriate most of the companies' holdings in Mexico, creating the foundation for Petróleos Mexicanos (PEMEX), Mexico's state-owned company. The government assessed the value of those holdings, which the firms also contested. The U.S. State Department did its own independent valuation of their worth and found the Mexican government's price to be generous and above their own appraisal. Before Cárdenas announced his decision on March 18, 1938, he was viewed by many groups in Mexico, including the Catholic hierarchy, the business community, religious Mexicans, and the political right, in a negative and controversial light. The day after his announcement, most Mexicans responded instantly, enthusiastically, and patriotically in support of the president's decision. Even the Catholic Church actively took up collections to help pay for the companies. As was the case elsewhere in Latin America and the Third World, the decision also increased feelings of nationalism. President José López Portillo (1976–82), a college student at that time, was influenced years later in his own decision to nationalize Mexico's banks by what happened in 1939. Cárdenas' political legacy following this decision made him Mexico's most popular president for the remainder of the twentieth century.

Did Mexico participate in World War II?

The relationship between Mexico and the United States immediately prior to World War II was often tense and difficult. President Cárdenas' decision to nationalize the petroleum industry in March 1939 only exacerbated these difficulties. Given its historical experience with U.S. intervention from the mid-nineteenth century, Mexico evolved a strong noninterventionist foreign policy posture in the post-revolutionary decades. Mexico, therefore, rarely pursued a leadership position in Latin American regional affairs, let alone wanted to become involved in international conflicts. When the Japanese forces attacked Pearl Harbor and the United States declared war on the Axis powers, the U.S. government viewed South America as a potential source of strong German influence and infiltration. Therefore, the border regions, and the desolate areas of Baja California, were considered to be potential threats to the U.S. security, including possible Japanese infiltration along the Pacific coast.

Unlike Brazil, which allowed the United States to use its territory as a base of operations for American Air Force flights to Africa that provided crucial logistical support for Allied forces against the Germans in North Africa, Mexico did not ally with the United States. Instead, Mexico maintained a low-key, but modestly collaborative attitude toward the United States. It focused increased attention within its Secretariat of National Defense on the northern military regions and brought former president and general Lázaro Cárdenas back on active duty to take charge of a regional military command. Mexico also accepted $39 million in lend-lease credits from the United States for improved training and weaponry. Near the end of the war, Mexico declared war on the Axis powers for attacking its oil tankers, which were transporting crude to America. It joined the United States by sending a small, expeditionary Air Force unit, the 201st Squadron, to participate in combat in the Philippines in 1945. That squadron became highly revered in Mexico, and many of its officers achieved the top posts in the Mexican Air Force. Instead of collaborating as a military ally of the United States for most of the war, Mexico's most useful and direct contribution was to provide human resources to the United States as a substitute for the manpower loss in unskilled jobs, including railroad track maintenance and agricultural harvesting. Mexico also acceded to requests from the United States to emphasize the production of certain goods that were needed for the war effort and could not be imported from traditional sources.

When did civilian leadership take control of the Mexican political system?

One of the most admirable achievements of the Mexican political model in the twentieth century was the ability of the political leadership to sustain continuous civilian control over the military, an accomplishment no other country in Latin America, with the exception of Costa Rica, attained. This remarkable achievement occurred incrementally after the Revolution of 1910. One way to measure the influence of military officers serving in national political office is to examine the percentage of first-time officeholders present in each administration. The data suggest several important patterns. The highest percentage occurred under Venustiano Carranza's 1914–20 administration, when 49 percent of the leading politicians were veteran officers. When General Obregón became president in 1920, 40 percent of national political figures were combat veterans. The presence of the officer corps in top posts continued at an average level of 30 percent during the reigns of presidents Calles, Portes Gil, Ortiz Rubio, and Rodríguez, from 1924 to 1934. All of these presidents, with the exception of the congressionally appointed interim president Portes Gil, were revolutionary generals.

Despite the fact that he was a general and leader of the victorious revolutionaries by 1929, General Calles, even while president, recognized the need to reduce the political role of the officer corps in Mexican politics. He reduced the number of high-ranking officers by a fourth, from 40 to 30 percent from that of his mentor and predecessor, General Obregón. He set in motion the professionalization of the officer corps, beginning a process of weeding out self-made generals with little or no formal military education. When Lázaro Cárdenas achieved the presidency in 1934 and independence from Calles in 1935, he believed the best way to keep the military under control was to incorporate it as one of four sectors in the recently created National Revolutionary Party (PNR). While half of the state governors continued to be military officers during his administration, he reduced career officers (excluding defense and navy) to only 12 percent of the cabinet posts. General Manuel Avila Camacho succeeded Cárdenas in the presidency in 1940, the last officer to achieve this position, and reversed Cárdenas' strategy, eliminating the military sector from the party structure. He too allowed the same small percentage of officers to serve in his cabinet and somewhat reduced their presence as governors. Civilian supremacy, however, truly dates from 1946, when Miguel Alemán became president, the first civilian to do so since Portes Gil. He eliminated all officers from the cabinet except in the two military ministries. He also nominated civilian governors, allowing only 13 percent of officers compared with 40 during his predecessor's administration, and only allowed 5 percent of the Senate to come from military backgrounds, the lowest figure until 1976. Although an important general competed actively for the presidency in 1952, civilian supremacy was already well entrenched.

What is the Alemán generation and what were its consequences for Mexican politics?

The Alemán generation refers to those politicians who collaborated with and came from the same generation as President Miguel Alemán (1946–52). This group of politicians is referred to collectively as the Alemán generation because they contributed numerous important and distinctive features to the evolving Mexican political model, features that determined leadership and political characteristics for decades to come. The most pronounced feature of this generation was its youth and its civilian origins. The Alemán generation, like the president himself, represented a new group of ambitious politicians born largely during the first decade of the twentieth century. They form the first post-revolutionary generation in that they typically did not serve in combat, they came from lower-middle and middle-class backgrounds, and they were well educated, most of them having graduated from preparatory school and college. Many of these younger political figures were prominent student leaders, having participated in the presidential campaign against Obregón's reelection in 1927–28, and again in favor of the candidacy of José Vasconcelos, a civilian who opposed the National Revolutionary Party's first official presidential candidate in the special election of 1929 to replace an interim president. No generation of politicians, before or since, has participated as actively in student politics as this group.

The Alemán generation also represented a political leadership that was the product of the increasing dominance of the National University of Mexico and the National Preparatory School, located in the capital, as well as the National School of Law. More than half of the president's generation graduated from the National University and nearly two-fifths from the National Preparatory School, figures which also have never been equaled before or since. The concentrated experiences of his generation in two educational institutions dramatically enhanced the importance of national, public educational institutions in the formation and recruitment of Mexican political leadership, and decreased the importance of other typical political institutions, such as parties, in playing that role. Finally, it can also be concluded that the Alemán generation, not that of Carlos Salinas, truly represents the first generation to introduce a technocratic leadership. Two-thirds of his collaborators were college graduates—a figure that was not equaled until the 1964–70 administration. By placing a high value on formal educational credentials, especially among assistant secretaries in the cabinet-level agencies, he increased the presence of politicians from middle-class social backgrounds and the importance of pursuing a career in the federal bureaucracy as the most important career track for upward political mobility during the PRI's reign.

What is the PRI?

The PRI refers to the Institutional Revolutionary Party, the party which dominated Mexican politics from 1929 through 2000. The PRI was the third version of the original National Revolutionary Party (PNR) founded by former President Calles and his collaborators in 1929. It was, in turn, reconstituted as the Party of the Mexican Revolution (PRM) in 1938 by President Cárdenas. On January 18, 1946, President Manuel Ávila Camacho decided to alter the party's name, designating it as the Institutional Revolutionary Party. The underlying rationale for making this name change was to suggest to the citizenry, as well as to the active PRI membership, that the Mexican state, and the party which represented it, had achieved an institutionalized phase of political development after the violent decade of the revolution. It is worth noting that the evolving name of the party only changed one word each time, from National, to Mexican, to Institutional.

These words are revealing about the attitudes of its leadership. In the first place, it was crucial to retain the word revolutionary in all three party names, given the fact that its leaders believed, and wanted to retain the image, that their party remained the only legitimate representative of the ideology of the revolution. They believed and succeeded for many years in giving the PRI and its antecedents an "official" linkage to the revolution and to the state. This attitude explains why many Mexicans referred to the PRI as the official party, as the government, and as the state. The acronym was used as a substitute for these concepts. The party reinforced this perception by choosing the three colors of the Mexican flag—green, white, and red—as its official partisan colors. Not only was this valuable in the visual images appearing during political campaigns, but also critical to numerous illiterate voters who used those colors to identify PRI candidates on the ballot.

The concern of the original founders to establish a truly national political party organization explains why the word National was used in combination with Revolution. After a decade, the reformed version, the Party of the Mexican Revolution, took on a more specific legitimizing term, suggesting again that it was the true party of the Mexican Revolution. That redesignation involved important structural changes in the organization of the party, designed to incorporate large numbers of partisans from various sectors of society. When President Ávila Camacho and party leaders altered the party's name for the final time, they wanted to reinforce the perception that the party's post-revolutionary achievements had become permanent, and that the party would provide stability and continuity into the future. President Carlos Salinas de Gortari (1988–94) considered changing the party's name again, but ultimately was persuaded to leave it untouched.

From 1946 through 1987, the party essentially functioned as a vehicle for maintaining itself in power, having monopolized most elective and appointive positions since the 1930s. From 1988 forward, it faced increasing electoral competition at all levels and went through numerous adjustments to transform itself into a competitive political party. Despite its major losses in the presidential elections of 2000 and 2006, it boasts the largest and broadest partisan base, making it the political force to reckon with in the future.

What is the Mexican economic miracle?

The Mexican economic miracle refers to the decades during which Mexico experienced its longest continuous period of sustained economic growth. Most observers date the so-called miracle from the late 1940s to the early 1970s, concentrated in four presidential administrations: Miguel Alemán (1946–52), Adolfo Ruiz Cortines (1952–58), Adolfo López Mateos (1958–64), and Gustavo Díaz Ordaz (1964–70). Economic growth during these years averaged a consistent 3 to 4 percent yearly and was characterized by low inflation rates. By the 1960s, gross domestic product was averaging 7 percent. Most economists attribute this growth to several important conditions. Most commonly, they point to the import substitution strategy pursued by the Mexican government, which protected domestic industry through high tariffs on consumer goods and allowed the importation of capital goods. The

administration of Miguel Alemán introduced and emphasized this industrialization strategy. Alemán and his succes-
sors expanded public investment in infrastructure and
transportation, and Mexico began rapidly to shift from a rural
to an urban society. It witnessed a huge internal shift in the
population from small villages and towns to urban centers, as
the percentage of Mexicans employed in agriculture declined
and those in manufacturing and services increased significantly. The second important explanation for this success is
that in the two decades preceding this growth, Mexico dramatically increased the number of children enrolled in school,
thus reducing illiteracy and enhancing the educational prep-
aration of the workforce.

While this period has been traditionally viewed in positive
terms because of the long-term growth in Mexico's gross
domestic product, careful studies by economists demonstrate
that contrary to popular perceptions, even though Mexico
increased the size of its economy and its productivity, most of
those economic benefits were not shared by the majority of
the economically active population. As late as 1994, more than
half of Mexico's population was classified by the United
Nations as living in poverty (i.e., earning less than $2 per
capita daily), and half of that population was classified as
living in absolute poverty (earning less than $1 per capita
daily). The contradictions between general economic growth,
the inequality in the distribution of that growth, and per
capita growth is reflected in the fact that Mexico was ranked
in 2009 as the 12th largest economy in the world but a mere
60th in per capita gross domestic product.

What is the PAN?

PAN is a leading political party that was founded in 1939 by
dissident politicians from the Mexican government and other
leading political activists searching for an ideological
alternative to the National Revolutionary Party (PNR)

founded by former president Calles and his collaborators in 1929. Its notable founders included Manuel Gómez Morín, a financial and political supporter of José Vasconcelos' opposition presidential campaign in 1929, and an influential contributor to Mexico's public financial institutions in the 1920s. The PAN was founded at the highpoint of Lázaro Cárdenas' administration. Many of its founders were opposed to policies implemented by Cárdenas and the direction of post-revolutionary governments. In particular they were critical of the government's orientation favoring the incorporation of socialist principles in public education, the anti-Catholic rhetoric of numerous government party officials, and, most significantly, the virtual political monopoly exercised by the Party of the Mexican Revolution (PNR's successor in 1938) over every elected office from mayor to president.

The PAN was Mexico's oldest opposition party until it won the presidential election in 2000. It grew very slowly under politically adverse circumstances at the state and local levels for decades. Its politicians and supporters were constantly harassed, and worse, sometimes killed during the 1940s, 1950s, and 1960s. It did not make significant headway against the PRI (which replaced the PRM in 1946) until the electoral reforms of 1964, which assigned a small number of "party seats" to the opposition parties in the Chamber of Deputies, Mexico's lower house. These positions, combined with a small number of congressional districts the PAN actually was able to win, allowed it to have a voice in the legislative branch and, importantly, to reward its party faithful with elected political offices. In the mid 1960s, its congressional candidates obtained 12 percent of the vote. By 2000, it earned more than 30 percent.

The PAN, in an attempt to maintain stronger ideological coherence, has kept its active party membership small, thus limiting its partisan base in an era of highly competitive elections since 1994. It also developed its electoral strength regionally rather than nationally and produced its greatest successes in urban centers in those areas. It lost ground in the 1988 presidential elections, when Cuauhtémoc Cárdenas obtained the second highest number of votes for president, but it made a comeback in 1994, winning a quarter of the votes for the presidency. More important, during the 1990s, it used its regional strengths and its pro-democratic ideology to increase its appeal at the state and local levels. By 1997, PAN, PRD and the smaller opposition parties represented 50 percent of the population at the state and local level, increasing that figure to 61 percent in 2001. The PAN has won the last two presidential contests and remains the incumbent party in the executive branch until 2012.

THE DECLINE OF THE PRI AND THE MEXICAN MODEL

What was the Tlatelolco student massacre of 1968 and what were its long-term political consequences?

On October 2, 1968, as a consequence of student protests at the National Autonomous University of Mexico (UNAM) and other public institutions (against the occupation of a vocational high school by police and also of UNAM by the army, violating the principle of university autonomy), thousands of students gathered at the Plaza of the Three Cultures in the Tlatelolco neighborhood of Mexico City for a peaceful demonstration against the government. The army was sent in to maintain order. Shots were fired from nearby apartment buildings, setting off a violent response from the troops surrounding the demonstration. Hundreds of students and bystanders were killed and wounded by the army, and in the aftermath hundreds of students, intellectuals, and professors were imprisoned by the government. Many years later it was revealed that President Gustavo Díaz Ordaz purposely provoked the violent response by sending snipers dressed in civilian clothes from his own presidential guard battalion to fire on army troops. Many analysts believe he pursued such a repressive strategy in part because the government had invested millions of dollars to sponsor the Olympic Games, scheduled to begin just ten days after the protest.

It is generally agreed that the events of 1968 became the most important catalyst for setting in motion a crisis of legitimacy for the Mexican government and the political model that had long been pursued by the incumbent Institutional Revolutionary Party (PRI). Not only did the government repression shock Mexicans from all social classes, it also tarnished its image abroad, especially in the United States. Most importantly, it set in motion numerous political consequences that ultimately contributed to a democratic transition in the 1980s and 1990s, and the defeat of the PRI in the presidential election of 2000.

The short- to medium-term consequences of the student massacre radicalized a generation of students who became political activists. Some of these individuals joined small leftist organizations. A number of these organizations eventually contributed to the expansion of the electoral left, serving as a partial basis of support for Cuauhtémoc Cárdenas' presidential campaign in 1988, and the establishment of the Party of the Democratic Revolution (PRD) in 1989. Other individuals joined peasant groups, participating in protests against the government, and some became involved with indigenous populations, including what became the Zapatista Army of National Liberation (EZLN) in Chiapas in 1994. Many Mexican intellectuals reacted strongly to the repression, encouraging some people to become more critical and independent of the state, and others to join or form opposition parties. Finally, in broad terms, the student repression encouraged the growth of civic organizations from all sectors of society, including businessmen, women, priests who were advocates of liberation theology, intellectuals, and others.

What was the "Dirty War" in Mexico?

Throughout South America during the 1970s and 1980s, the military and their conservative civilian allies were engaged in a violent conflict against leftist political groups for control of their respective political systems. Many individuals involved in this struggle viewed the leftist opposition as a threat to their country's civilization and survival. With the help of the armed forces, these groups set in motion repressive, authoritarian regimes that committed horrific human rights abuses, during which many people disappeared from their homes or off the street. Thus, scholars referred to these events as a "dirty war" and the victims as "the disappeared." Mexico experienced its own "Dirty War," but it never was as deeply or widely entrenched as elsewhere in the region, nor did it involve the armed forces taking control of the political apparatus either directly or indirectly. The persecution of left-wing political activists, or individuals often only remotely linked to such activists through friendship or family, began in earnest after the 1968 student movement.

After imprisoning many activists following the tragic massacre of students and bystanders in October 1968, the government instructed its security forces to persecute other potential leaders. In December 1970, President Luis Echeverría, the former minister of government who oversaw the massacre of student demonstrators under his predecessor, took office and began his own contradictory strategy of dealing with dissident groups. He recruited some former student leaders to the government and pursued others through the Federal Security Agency in the Secretariat of Government or directly through the armed forces. A number of groups resisted the violent reprisals, and several guerrilla organizations came into existence during the Echeverría administration (1979–76).

The most notable guerrilla movement in opposition to government policies during this era was that of Lucio Cabañas, a former rural school teacher from a peasant family. Cabañas was a leader of the National Federation of Peasant Societies, a group independent of the government, and eventually organized a guerrilla movement in the poor southern state of Guerrero. The movement operated from 1968 until 1974, when Cabañas was killed under mysterious circumstances by army forces. During this period, units of the Mexican Army were involved in human rights abuses throughout Mexico, including the murder of prisoners. They killed prisoners by tossing them out of airplanes and more commonly by executing them at military bases, notably at Military Base No. 1 in Mexico City. Only two general officers were ever tried for such abuses after the National Action Party came to power in 2000, and although genocide charges were brought against former president Echeverría, he was never convicted.

What was the impact of the 1964 electoral reforms?

In the second half of the twentieth century, the Institutional Revolutionary Party, facing increasing criticism of its semi-authoritarian political model, decided to introduce electoral reforms that altered the distribution of majority districts and added what became known as party deputies to the federal legislative branch. Prior to the reforms, the lower house of congress, the Chamber of Deputies, consisted of 178 congressional districts. Between 1949 and 1961, the PRI only lost thirty-three out of a total of 807 district seats. In 1964, it decided to alter the composition of the congressional seats, introducing an additional thirty-six to forty-one party deputy seats during the congressional sessions from 1964 to 1979. The law relied on a formula based on the percentage of votes cast for congressional candidates in each election. The underlying rationale the PRI used for introducing this change was to create the impression that the electoral system was more democratic and competitive than was actually the case, assigning these seats only to opposition party candidates. For example, in the 1964 elections, in addition to the 178 seats assigned to the victorious candidate in each congressional district, of which the PRI won 175 districts (fairly or through fraud), thirty-six additional seats were assigned to three other parties. The majority of those seats were allocated to the National Action Party up to 1979. In 1977, President José López Portillo passed new legislation, which not only increased the number of majority districts to three hundred seats, but also created a plurinominal system to replace the party deputy system, allocating one hundred additional seats, a fourth of all congressional seats, to the new plurinominal system. Years later, an additional one hundred plurinominal seats were added, bringing the total to five hundred seats, the current number in the Chamber of Deputies.

The 1964 reforms creating the party deputy system (which ultimately became the plurinominal system) produced a significant, long-term impact on the composition of the legislative branch and on the composition of party leadership in the opposition parties, particularly on the PAN, which was the first opposition party to defeat the PRI for the presidency in 2000. Because the PAN could not elect many of its most active and notable partisan supporters to the majority districts, the leadership of the party designated candidates who would receive the party or plurinominal seats. This process centralized control over the nominations in the hands of the party bureaucracy in Mexico City, thus inhibiting the more rapid development of regional and municipal party affiliates who could promote successful candidates to the only national offices PAN politicians could win: seats in the legislative branch. Those legal changes helped institutionalize the importance of PAN leadership and the national party bureaucracy from the Federal District.

What were the leading political characteristics of Mexico's semi-authoritarian model?

As Mexico began to evolve its unique and often successful political model from the 1930s through the 1980s, it developed a number of qualities that not only characterized it but also explain, in part, its longevity. The most important of those qualities included: a self-perpetuating political elite that represented each generation of younger politicians; a civilian leadership that institutionalized its supremacy and control over the military and the revolutionary veterans; a pragmatic ideology that legitimized itself in the rhetoric of the 1910 Revolution; the establishment of a corporatist system that linked the most populous occupational groups to the federal government and the party; a strong national party that served as an electoral vehicle; and the legitimacy of the presidency, reinforced by rejecting the concept of reelection, consecutive or otherwise.

The leadership of the PRI and its antecedent parties and the federal government developed a process by which they were able to satisfy a broad group of ambitious politicians and a wide range of ideologies, incorporating them and rewarding them with government posts in all three branches of government and in all levels, local, state, and national. The president was at the apex of this system and exercised the greatest influence over nominees for elective office and appointees for top posts in the judicial and executive branches. With the advent of the generation of President Miguel Alemán (1946–52), a post-revolutionary group of civilian lawyers took control of the national and state political system, and dramatically reduced the influence of combat veterans and professional military officers on the political system, establishing a firm benchmark for civilian control from 1946 to the present. The government and party leadership was more pragmatic than ideological, creating a broad ideological umbrella under which they could invite talented and ambitious politicians to join forces with their collaborators. The leadership, beginning with President Lázaro Cárdenas, encouraged labor and peasant organizations to develop formal ties with the party and the government, cementing a relationship that remains to some extent today with the PRI. It also created nonvoluntary business organizations that channeled private sector demands to appropriate federal agencies. It developed an effective, grassroots electoral organization whose primary goal was to keep the PRI and its supporters in power, rather than to take power away from other political organizations. Finally, it assigned significant informal powers to the presidency, further legitimating its control and influence over the entire political model, creating an expectation, which remains in part to the present, that the president should exercise power firmly and definitively.

What were the consequences of the nationalization of the banks in 1982?

During the presidency of Luis Echeverría, the Mexican government began acquiring an increasing number of businesses ranging from fertilizer companies to restaurants. From 1972 through the end of the decade state ownership of private firms tripled. At the end of his administration, Echeverría took over agricultural properties in northwest Mexico, alienating the private sector. When his successor, José López Portillo, took office in 1976, he made an effort to reestablish positive relations with the private sector. During the early part of his administration, he was successful in achieving that goal. But as Mexico's economic situation became more difficult later in his term, provoked by the dramatic decline in oil prices, on which the government under both administrations had become increasingly dependent, wealthy Mexicans began taking their funds out of the country and depositing or investing them in the United States. After consulting only with two of his collaborators, López Portillo surprised the Mexican public, fellow politicians, and the private sector with his decision to nationalize all the banks. Unlike the decision to nationalize the petroleum industry, the banks were Mexican-owned. The president publicly blamed the bankers for not preventing capital from fleeing the country. This decision reversed all of the president's prior efforts to strengthen the relationship between the government and the private sector. Interestingly, however, a poll taken shortly after the nationalization revealed that most small- and medium-businesses outside the banking sector reacted favorably to the government taking over the management of the banks, a reaction explained by the fact that most large banks belonged to large holding companies representing other economic sectors and that they typically gave preference to firms owned by their own holding company when making loans. It has been estimated that indirectly, through mortgages controlled by the banks, the government controlled 80 to 85 percent of the economy.

The long-term impact of this decision resulted in a difficult period in the relationship between the private sector and the government. This relationship was repaired substantially by Miguel de la Madrid (1982–88), who returned some of the insurance companies acquired through the nationalization to the private sector at the end of his administration. Still, some members of the private sector and several of the leading business organizations became much more politically active in opposing the government and its economic policies, setting the stage in the 1990s for businessmen to become involved in electoral politics, typically in support of the PAN. De la Madrid chose Carlos Salinas de Gortari as his successor, and as part of his neo-liberal economic strategy, Salinas sold off all of the banks to the prominent capitalists. In the long run, however, ownership of these banks shifted to foreign companies, which presently control more than 90 percent of banking firms in Mexico.

Did Mexico's economic woes in the 1980s have significant political consequences?

Mexico's long-term reliance on an import substitution strategy, heavy spending of revenues from the sale of the state-owned petroleum companies, and excessive borrowing of monies from United States and European banks led to a major economic crisis in the last few months of the López Portillo administration (1976–82), shortly before the inauguration of President Miguel de la Madrid in December 1982. Mexico was forced to suspend payments on its foreign debt, and the new president decided to adopt severe austerity measures. Gross domestic product (adjusted for inflation) had increased an average of 8.4 percent yearly from 1977 to 1981, but collapsed to an incredible 0.1 percent during the entirety of the de la Madrid administration from 1982 to 1988—which witnessed rates of inflation averaging 88 percent during the same time period. The government's austerity measures, including economic pacts with organized labor and the private sector, limited social spending, severely restricted wage increases, and increased prices for basic commodities, producing a drop in real wages of nearly 50 percent from 1982 to 1988.

There was talk in the Mexican media during 1983–84 of the increased potential for social violence, given the breadth and depth of the impact of the economic crisis on the average Mexican's standard of living. The economic crisis and the government's policy solutions contributed to three significant, longer-term consequences. First, it further delegitimized the Mexican political model, which had relied heavily on long periods of economic growth in the early administrations to retain control. It also encouraged an increase in independent labor organizations and a decline in organized labor as a percentage of the overall economically active population. Second, combined with the federal government's inept reaction to a devastating earthquake in Mexico City in 1985, the austerity program encouraged hundreds of nongovernmental organizations to emerge, leading to a dramatic growth in civic organizations, which presented growing demands to the government. This development also encouraged the direct involvement of women in social movements, laying the groundwork for political opposition to the system and a gradual democratic transition. Third and finally, the government leadership, in response to the severity of the crisis, decided to pursue a neo-liberal economic policy solution based upon a trade-led economic strategy and a trading bloc with the United States and Canada (NAFTA), a strategy which continues to be pursued by the current administration.

9

MEXICO'S DEMOCRATIC TRANSITION

How did Carlos Salinas alter the Mexican political model?

Carlos Salinas de Gortari became president of Mexico in 1988, after a highly contentious and fraudulent election. His predecessor, Miguel de la Madrid, selected his former secretary of Programming and Budgeting to continue his own economic philosophy, reflecting an internationally oriented, neo-liberal strategy. To reinforce that policy direction, Salinas surrounded himself with political technocrats who, similar to the president, often had undergraduate degrees in economics, rarely had electoral political experience, boasted advanced graduate education abroad, typically at Ivy League schools in the United States, and introduced an increasing number of graduates from private universities in the capital, especially from the Autonomous Technological Institute of Mexico (ITAM), to top political posts.

Salinas, in pursuing the altered economic strategy, made significant changes in the political landscape, which inadvertently created a positive setting for a democratic transition from the one-party dominance of the PRI. Among the changes he made, four stand out for their impact on the historic semi-authoritarian model. First and most strongly linked to his economic philosophy, he sought to integrate Mexico to a new economic bloc to increase its competitiveness in the global economy, proposing a North American Free Trade Agreement (NAFTA) with the United States, its largest trading partner, and Canada. In completing the NAFTA treaty during his last year in office, Salinas moved Mexico away, for the first time, from an isolationist political posture in the region to multiple international influences, including increased attention from various institutions and constituencies in the United States. These influences eventually had an impact in encouraging democratization within Mexico. Second, on his own initiative, and in part to bring Mexico into the end of the twentieth century in terms of its international human rights agreements (which contradicted constitutional restrictions on clergy in Mexico), he eliminated a number of provisions regarding state-church relations, even though his action was opposed by many members of his own party. The elimination of these long-time restrictions encouraged more activist bishops and clergy to publicly support civic organizations and electoral democracy through numerous diocesan missives. Third, in order to cultivate support from Wall Street and from the U.S. Senate, he altered the outcome of some important state elections, including races for governor, permitting the first victory of an opposition party candidate to win a governorship since 1929, sixty years after the party was founded. These state and local victories encouraged the growth of both the National Action Party and the Party of the Democratic Revolution. Fourth, his excessive reliance on bureaucratic technocrats from the PRI, rather than on politicians with roots in elective offices and party organizations, produced a reaction within the PRI. The party changed its own internal rules to require that its presidential candidate have electoral and party experience, encouraging an important shift favoring a generation of politicians with such credentials and preparing the PRI in the long run for participation in a comparative electoral setting.

Why is the presidential election of 1988 a benchmark for democracy in Mexico?

To many analysts and students of Mexican politics, 1988 will remain a significant starting point in Mexico's transition to electoral democracy. That year is significant to the PRI itself because it was the first presidential election year since 1952 that a prominent individual active in the party became a significant opposition party candidate. By 1986, leading politicians within the PRI who held ambitions to become their party's presidential candidate realized that President Miguel de la Madrid was going to pursue a neo-liberal economic strategy that was opposed by the traditional wing of the party. This wing included Cuauhtémoc Cárdenas, the former governor of Michoacán and son of Mexico's most popular president, Lázaro Cárdenas, and Porfirio Muñoz Ledo, a former president of the PRI. These two figures, along with other leading members of the party, formed a "Democratic Current" within the party and ultimately were forced out of the PRI, taking a number of prominent politicians with them. When Carlos Salinas de Gortari was designated the PRI candidate, a number of smaller leftist parties obtained recognition and ran against him, as did the National Action Party, the most popular opposition party until 1988. Although Cárdenas formed his own party, the Cardenista Front for National Reconstruction, to support his candidacy, he was eventually listed on the ballot under four different parties.

Salinas was not a popular choice among many PRI faithful, thus giving Cárdenas a more viable opportunity as an opposition candidate. He campaigned vigorously, having widespread name recognition because of his father's reputation. When the election was held, the PRI resorted to outright fraud to alter the vote totals for the three leading candidates after discovering that Salinas was not obtaining even a simple majority of votes. Although some observers believe that Cárdenas won the election, the polling data suggest that

Salinas likely won with a much smaller margin of votes. What is most important about the results, however, is that for the first time since the 1930s, Mexican voters could understand that it actually might be possible to defeat the PRI. In short, the 1988 election became a victory for all opposition parties, strengthening increased political opposition at the state and local levels. One year later, the PAN won the first gubernatorial race since the PRI came to power. The 1988 election also led to the formation of a third significant party in Mexican politics, the Party of the Democratic Revolution (PRD), which nearly won the presidency in the 2006 elections. Through the PRD, the 1988 election strengthened the Mexican left, and in spite of continuous divisions within the PRD, increased the left's unity in the electoral arena.

Who is Cuauhtémoc Cárdenas and what is the PRD?

Cuauhtémoc Cárdenas Solórzano is a Mexican politician who comes from an influential political family, beginning with his father, General Lázaro Cárdenas, president of Mexico from 1934–40. To many Mexicans, his father symbolized a defender of Mexican sovereignty, after nationalizing foreign oil companies in 1939. He also symbolized agrarian reform, after distributing more land to peasants than any previous president. Cuauhtémoc began his political career as a student supporter of General Miguel Henríquez Guzmán's presidential campaign in 1951 and helped support his father's leadership of the National Liberation Movement in the 1960s. He was elected senator from his home state of Michoacán before becoming governor, following in the footsteps of his father and uncle. After leaving office, he joined other prominent PRI politicians in founding the Democratic Current in 1986, a faction within the party which supported the anti-neo-liberal economic strategy being pursued by President de la Madrid as well as increased political pluralism. When Carlos Salinas de Gortari was selected as the PRI's candidate, it became clear that the neo-liberal policies would be continued. Cárdenas and other leading members of the Democratic Current left the PRI and formed their own small party, and Cárdenas became the party's presidential candidate in 1988. Eventually he was supported by four small parties. In the hard-fought campaign that ensued, Cárdenas officially won 37 percent of the vote to Salinas' 51 percent, and the National Action Party candidate obtained 17 percent in an election marred by fraud. (See other entry in Chapter 9.)

Most observers believe that Cárdenas won a larger percentage of the vote, and some believe he possibly may have defeated Salinas. Nevertheless, even though Cárdenas lost, his electoral success gave birth in 1989 to a new, influential opposition party, the Party of the Democratic Revolution. Cárdenas presided over the party from 1989 to 1993, when he became the party's candidate a second time in the 1994 election, losing against the PRI candidate Ernesto Zedillo. The PRD was an amalgam of left-of-center parties and numerous defectors from the PRI who favored increased pluralization, fair elections, and a return to a state-supported system of increased social expenditures. Cárdenas' success also increased opposition party representation in congress. The establishment of the PRD encouraged alliances between it and the PAN on the state level, leading to successful gubernatorial campaigns which continue to the present. The strength of the PRD and PAN in Congress forced significant changes in the electoral process instituted in 1996, contributing to an independent institution, the Federal Electoral Institute, exercising complete control over the elections and providing public funding for all parties. Although Cárdenas unsuccessfully ran a third time for president in 2000, placing a distant third behind the PAN and PRI candidates, the party recovered its strength through the leadership of Andrés Manuel López Obrador, who presided over the PRD and the Mexico City government before narrowly losing against Felipe Calderón in the 2006 presidential race.

What is NAFTA and how did Carlos Salinas change Mexico's economic model?

When Carlos Salinas de Gortari became president of Mexico in 1988, he did not have a clear electoral mandate, having won the election through extensive fraud. In order to establish a greater level of legitimacy and support, he pursued a number of decisive political actions in the first six months of his administration. But his most significant, long-term strategy, which was innovative and controversial, was to stimulate Mexico's economic growth by expanding its global economic ties through the establishment of an economic trade bloc. It became apparent to economists and political leaders worldwide that most countries needed to associate themselves with other countries in order to compete globally. Salinas, who believed strongly in this concept, initially approached the European Economic Union. But the European Economic Union was overwhelmed with integrating those countries that were part of the former Soviet Union and turned him down. As a result, he then decided to propose to the United States and Canada the formation of a North American free trade agreement, which would reduce tariffs on the importation of hundreds of goods among the three countries. It was a controversial proposal within Mexico and in the United States. Indeed, it became an issue in the 1992 U.S. presidential campaign, during which independent candidate Ross Perot strongly criticized the concept. But Salinas, relying on a close working relationship with President George H. Bush, effectively lobbied Congress and Wall Street, stifling opposition to the proposal within his own party and censoring independent criticism. He eventually succeeded in achieving an agreement that formally went into effect January 1, 1994.

In addition to implementing NAFTA, he complemented his global economic strategy with a reversal of government ownership of many enterprises and the banks, which were nationalized by President José López Portillo in 1982. His administration sold off numerous companies and banks, many to favored individuals, restoring control to the private sector and reestablishing better relations between the private sector and the government. This domestic and international economic strategy produced increased capital investment in Mexico from abroad, and dramatically increased Mexican exports to its preferred trading partners. At the same time, however, many Mexicans lost their jobs, as cheaper imports from the United States put small entrepreneurs out of business. Unlike in the United States, which allocated funds to retrain Americans who also became unemployed, those Mexicans had to fend for themselves.

Finally, Salinas introduced an entirely new concept of federal assistance to local communities, through an agency called Pronasol. Essentially, Pronosal became a distributive entity through which federal revenues were directly distributed to local communities for projects desired by those communities. The president travelled on hundreds of work trips to small municipalities during his administration to personally meet local leaders and allocate these funds. Although critics charged that the funds were used to generate legitimacy for the PRI government, more than half of the funds went directly to local communities. This strategy revived the importance of munici-palities and served as an underlying basis of more specific anti-poverty programs undertaken by presidents Zedillo and Fox.

Who are the technocrats?

In general terms, technocrats refer to individuals, typically professional people, with specialized skills and advanced education. In Latin America, primarily in the Southern Cone, the word refers to economists who pursued a macro-economic policy strategy in line with the conservative economic views propounded at the University of Chicago. In Mexico, the term technocrats takes on a different and somewhat unique definition. Most analysts view technocrats as a special type of Mexican politician who emerged in top leadership positions in the federal executive branch beginning in the early 1980s. The first Mexican president who can be viewed as a technocrat is Miguel de la Madrid, a graduate of the National School of Law, who completed an MA degree in public administration from Harvard University. De la Madrid was responsible for encouraging a new type of politician to hold cabinet posts and important offices in the subcabinet, especially in economically oriented agencies ranging from trade to agriculture to the treasury. Among his most prominent appointees were Carlos Salinas de Gortari, his budget and programming secretary, and Jesús Silva Herzog, his initial treasury secretary. Both men were graduates of the National School of Economics, both obtained advanced degrees in the United States at Harvard and Yale respectively, both men pursued political careers in the federal bureaucracy, and both men had never held elective office.

The selection of de la Madrid, Carlos Salinas, and Ernesto Zedillo, the last three PRI presidents, reinforced all the characteristics mentioned above. All three men served in the programming and budgeting cabinet post (which was combined with treasury under Salinas), making it the most affording post for a Mexican politician with presidential ambitions. The technocrats, having trained in the United States, returned to Mexico with the belief that neo-liberal economic strategies, similar to those pursued in the United States, were the long-term solution to Mexico's economic and social problems. The presence of these individuals, who shared similar career characteristics and beliefs about Mexico development policies, reached their apex under Ernesto Zedillo (1994–2000). As a faction within the Institutional Revolutionary Party, they were opposed by those politicians who held different economic views, and who typically were trained in more traditional disciplines and had pursued careers in the electoral arena and the party bureaucracy.

Although de la Madrid has been identified as the first tech-nocratic president, a careful examination of presidential administrations reveals that Miguel Alemán and his gener-ation are the historical antecedents of many similar qualities, anticipating the economist technocrat by nearly forty years. Also, it is apparent that a new generation of technocrats, born in the 1960s but who share somewhat different qualities, have emerged in the Calderón administration. Their future influence remains unknown.

When did an opposition party win its first governorship in Mexico?

The answer to this question always must be qualified because it is likely that on several occasions opposition candidates won gubernatorial elections in their respective states, but were not recognized as victors because of PRI-initiated fraud at the ballot box. The most notable historical example of this occurred in San Luis Potosi as early as 1961, when Salvador Nava Martínez, a popular, politically active physician, ran against the PRI candidate for governor after being rejected by the PRI as a nominee. He ran as the candidate of the Potosino Civic Front, but was declared the loser in an election marred by widespread fraud. He was later arrested and imprisoned for political reasons in the 1960s. Three decades later he ran again as a gubernatorial candidate in 1991 representing an alliance of opposition parties, including the PAN, after having won the mayoralty election in the state capital of San Luis Potosí in 1982. Again, the PRI committed widespread fraud in the election. After the PRI governor had held office for less than two weeks, following a protest march organized by Nava, President Salinas forced the governor to resign, but replaced him with another PRI politician instead of Nava.

The first opposition governor who won a gubernatorial election recognized by the government was Ernesto Ruffo Appel, who took office in Baja California on November 1, 1989, setting in motion the beginning of a wave of opposition victories by the National Action Party, and to a lesser extent, the Party of the Democratic Revolution, on the state level. Ruffo's victory was critical in convincing voters that gubernatorial candidates from other parties could indeed win an election, and therefore deserved their serious consideration and votes as potential candidates. Ruffo, typical of a new generation of PAN politicians, came from a business background, had served as mayor of Ensenada from 1986 to 1988, and led local business organizations. He later served in President Fox's cabinet.

What was the Zapatista uprising of 1994 and what were its political consequences?

On January 1, 1994, a small guerrilla band of indigenous Mexicans in the poor southern state of Chiapas attacked several army posts in what became known as the Zapatista uprising. The North American Free Trade Agreement (NAFTA) with the United States and Canada formally went into effect on that date, and they used it as a symbol, in opposition to the neo-liberal economic policies of the Salinas administration. The brief and militarily ineffective uprising was put down violently by the Mexican armed forces, which committed human rights abuses in defeating the poorly armed guerrillas. Formally known as the Zapatista National Liberation Army (EZLN), the peasants who made up the members of the guerrillas, and their active supporters, had a long list of complaints against local, state, and federal authorities. They advocated agrarian reforms and opposed Salinas' revisions of the agrarian provisions in Article 27 of the Constitution. They also believed they had been effectively excluded from the political process, and they viewed their economic situation as continuing to deteriorate compared with most other Mexicans.

Militarily, the Zapatistas proved to be unsuccessful. Politically, however, most Mexicans were favorably predisposed to their goals, although they were opposed to their initial use of violence. The Zapatistas used the Internet effectively, both in Mexico and the United States, to gain support, and they were equally effective in finding allies in the domestic and international media. They exercised a long-term political impact in two ways. First, and most influential, they served as a catalyst for the establishment and activity of dozens of nongovernmental organizations that pressed their own social and economic demands on the government. These groups, along with the EZLN, which transformed itself into a vociferous political organization, contributed to the growth of civic organizations and to widespread support for the democratic transition of the Mexican political system. Second, although the Zapatistas never formally achieved an agreement with the Mexican government, and they have exercised little influence on the political arena in recent years, they did initiate a broader movement, found elsewhere in the region, in favor of indigenous rights and municipal autonomy in Mexico.

What were the consequences of the Zapatistas for civil-military relations?

When the Zapatista National Liberation Army attacked several army installations on the morning of January 1, 1994, in part to symbolize their objection to the North American Free Trade Agreement and what it implied for Mexican peasants, it produced numerous consequences for the Mexican armed forces, for the relationship between civil and military authorities, and for the military's role in determining national security policy. The uprising caught the Mexican public and the international community completely by surprise. (See the immediately preceding question.) As was the case some twenty-five years earlier when troops surrounded the student demonstrators in Tlatelolco Plaza in 1968, the army was asked to react to a difficult political problem created by civilian leaders' incompetence. The events of January 1994, however, were even more consequential for the civil-military relationship because military intelligence for more than a year previous to these events had warned civilian agencies of the disenchantment of these groups and their future actions against local authorities.

The armed forces' immediate suppression of the small guerrilla bands was brutal and involved widely reported human rights violations, presenting the military in a negative light in the domestic and international media. Officers within the armed forces became disgruntled with civilian security leadership and decision-making, ultimately pressuring national leadership to include the secretariats of national defense and navy in the decision-making process, thus allowing the military to have a voice in those policies they would be asked to enforce or implement. As a consequence, they became an effective voice in the national security sub-cabinet. Equally important, military dissatisfaction with their role in controlling the Zapatistas led to a unique, highly critical self-appraisal within the military in a 1995 internal memorandum that was leaked to the Mexican media. This report identified numerous institutional weaknesses and outlined concrete strategies for improvement. Many could be traced to their role in suppressing the Zapatista uprising. For example, the report recommended a complete overhaul of the military's electronic capabilities, including advanced training in computer technology and the acquisition of superior computer equipment. This recommendation, in part, was a response to the Zapatistas' successful use of the Internet in presenting their case to the public and to the international media and scholarly community. The report also recommended that the armed forces improve their intelligence gathering efforts and establish links with counterpart civilian agencies, such as the attorney general of Mexico. Finally, the report recommended the expansion of mobile units that could be flown into difficult security situations, giving the army increased logistical flexibility.

Why is the presidential election of 1994 considered a second benchmark in the democratic transition?

In the presidential race of 1988, Cuauhtémoc Cárdenas clearly demonstrated in an election wrought with government fraud that he could win at least 37 percent of the vote, suggesting that the next presidential election in 1994 would become a test of whether or not Mexican voters would rally behind an appealing opposition candidate. In 1994, the three leading parties were the Institutional Revolutionary Party (PRI), which chose Luis Donaldo Colosio, Salinas' secretary of social development, former president of PRI, and a past member of the Chamber of Deputies and the Senate (and the first PRI candidate in thirty years to have held elective office); the Party of the Democratic Revolution (PRD), which ran Cárdenas for his second attempt at the presidency; and the National Action Party (PAN), which chose Diego Fernández del Cevallos, a federal deputy, a member of the PAN National Executive Committee, and a leading lawyer. The PRI confronted serious political difficulties after the Zapatista uprising took place (shortly after the race began) and, seven weeks later, when Colosio, the PRI candidate, was shockingly assassinated while campaigning in Tijuana. Confronted by Constitutional restrictions on the amount of time a candidate must resign any public office before his election, Salinas, with few supporters in the party apparatus, was forced to select Ernesto Zedillo, his former education secretary and Colosio's campaign manager.

Unlike the 1988 election, however, the 1994 election took place under different electoral laws. These laws assigned sole responsibility for the election to the Federal Electoral Institute, increased the election's transparency, incorporated international observers on Election Day, and received constant coverage in published public opinion polls. The election was considered by leading analysts to have been mostly free of fraud. Thus 1994 became a test to see if the PRI could maintain its incumbent status, or if the opposition could succeed in defeating Zedillo. Citizen beliefs in the fairness and importance of the election, given the political instability brought on by the Zapatista uprising and the assassination of the PRI candidate, were demonstrated on Election Day. It saw the highest turnout of registered voters, 78 percent, ever recorded before or since. The PRI won with 50 percent of the vote, surprising analysts, and the PAN replaced the PRD as the second most important party, winning 26 percent of the vote. The elections demonstrated the competitiveness of the parties and confirmed citizen beliefs that they were fair. The PRI actually benefited from the perceived political instability among some voters, who preferred to vote for the incumbent party rather than to make a drastic change in leadership. The strong showing of the opposition parties in the chamber of deputies produced further electoral reforms that guaranteed an even playing field in the 2000 presidential election. In the 2000 election the opposition finally won with a plurality of votes.

What was the role of the Catholic Church in the 1994 presidential race?

No institution has been as significantly ignored by analysts for its role in the transformation of the Mexican electoral process specifically and the democratic transition broadly than that of the Catholic clergy. In spite of important inroads by evangelical Protestants in the 1980s and 1990s, 85 percent of the population still identifies itself as Catholic. The majority of those individuals actively practice their faith by attending mass. More importantly, the Mexican public, in survey after survey, consistently gives the Church as an institution its highest level of confidence, along with that of educational institutions and schoolteachers, compared with all other institutions. Some Mexicans even expect clergy to take positions on nonspiritual matters, including secular social, economic, and political issues. Thus Catholic clergy, through public

statements and its involvement in religiously affiliated organizations which claim the largest membership of any type of
organizations in Mexico including labor unions, exercise the
potential for having an impact on Mexican political values
and preferences.

The 1917 Constitution strictly prohibits ministers representing any religion from using the pulpit to promote partisan political preferences. This prohibition is rarely violated
in practice; instead the Catholic hierarchy since the 1980s has
issued important public statements through individual dio-
ceses advocating civic responsibility in exercising the right to
vote, and reinforcing the Church's support for democratic
institutions and free elections. As public interest grew in the
1994 election, the Catholic Church took a proactive posture in
advocating that each Mexican had a personal responsibility to
vote. Indeed, it went so far to say that registered voters who
were not exercising their voting rights were committing a sin.
We will never know for sure the extent to which Catholic
bishops and priests influenced the turnout for the 1994
election, but there is no question that they made a difference
in the level of turnout. They also played an important role in
educating voters to judge candidates on their stated beliefs
and credentials rather than on the basis of their party affiliation. Six years later, in the 2000 presidential race, they
repeated their position on the importance of voting, while
simultaneously condemning candidates who used fear of
change as reason for maintaining the status quo, as antidemocratic and sinful.

What were the consequences of the assassination of the PRI presidential candidate Luis Donaldo Colosio in 1994?

In late March 1994, well into the presidential election campaign,
the Institutional Revolutionary Party (PRI) candidate, Luis
Donaldo Colosio, was assassinated in Tijuana, Baja California.
Since 1929, no Mexican president, presidential candidate, or

candidate-elect had been murdered. Consequently, the death of Colosio came as a great shock to the Mexican public and political class, and was viewed as a second destabilizing event coming on the heels of the violent uprising by the Zapatistas in the first week of January of that same year. Both events received significant attention from the international media as well as from Mexican domestic sources. (See question on the presidential election of 1994 in this chapter.) Colosio's untimely death produced consequences for the larger electoral process, and, equally important, for internal conditions inside the PRI leadership.

The broader impact was to reinforce the views of certain voters who were fearful of supporting opposition candidates in a time of perceived political instability. Voters who were affected by this perception were more likely to vote for the replacement PRI presidential candidate, thus affecting the outcome of the presidential election and delaying an ultimate test of electoral democracy, that of changing control from one political party to another. On the other hand, Colosio's murder led to decisions that made it obvious to all Mexicans and outside observers that the PRI's mechanism for choosing its presidential nominee was clearly authoritarian. With the election taking place the first week of July, President Salinas was forced to choose between the president of the PRI and the manager of Colosio's campaign, Ernesto Zedillo, a former member of the president's cabinet. The choice of Zedillo produced several important consequences within the party, all of which contributed to the democratic transition. Zedillo himself, after being elected president, did not resort to the dictatorial process used by all of his predecessors to designate his successor. Instead, he encouraged the party to develop a primary system to select its candidate, and for the only time in its history, the party conducted an open presidential primary for its nominee in 2000, setting an example for other parties. Moreover, the designation of Zedillo, who had no prior history of party or elective positions in his background, produced significant internal reforms within party leadership who wished to promote the candidacies of PRI figures boasting just such credentials. These electoral and party credentials have since become the norm among the candidates of all three parties for governors and presidents.

How did President Zedillo contribute to the democratic transition?

Throughout his campaign, President Ernesto Zedillo, the last PRI president, promised to make changes that would contribute to strengthening the rule of law, and, once in office, he initiated important changes that affected the outcome of the 2000 presidential race. He used his executive authority to carry out an important reform to the supreme court, Mexico's highest judicial body, and those changes, in 1995, set in motion the basis for a more independent judiciary. He essentially established a limit of fifteen years for justices, or less if they reached mandatory retirement age. Under the reforms, the president would present a candidate for open positions, but a two-thirds majority in the Senate would have to approve his choice. Furthermore, as had often been the case previously, appointees were not allowed to have held a public office one year prior to their appointment. The reformed court also could rule for the first time on the constitutionality of laws. Shortly after the new justices took office and the reforms were enacted, the court made several major rulings against the executive branch, demonstrating its independence.

Even more important to the democratic transition, however, were changes Zedillo's administration instituted in the electoral laws, making the Federal Electoral Institute and Federal Electoral Court completely independent bodies, and creating an even political playing field through public funding of all recognized political parties. In the elections for 2000, for example, the National Action Party and its allies, campaigning on a joint ticket for president, actually received more funds than did the PRI. Zedillo also made a major change within his own party, instructing the party to create a primary system to select the PRI's presidential nominee, the first time in its history that the candidate was not chosen by the incumbent or former president. The PRI decided to institute an open primary where any registered voter could participate in the designation of its candidate. This is the only case to date among the three leading parties of an open, general primary for a presidential candidate. Finally, and perhaps most important of all, when the exit polls showed Fox the clear winner, despite the fact that the Federal Electoral Institute did not have complete results, the president went on television to congratulate Fox, the National Action Party candidate, for his victory, legitimizing his election and the victory before all Mexicans. Some analysts also believe that by doing so, President Zedillo headed off any attempt by PRI tradition-alists to alter the electoral outcome. President Zedillo should be viewed as a president who encouraged democratic change and helped to legitimize a competitive, democratic process.

What is the Mexican bailout?

When Ernesto Zedillo took office on December 1, 1994, he and his economic team decided that it was necessary to devalue the Mexican peso against the dollar. During the Salinas administration (1988–94), the government had allowed the peso to become heavily overvalued. Zedillo's advisers recom-mended that Mexico allow demand for the peso in the inter-national market to determine its value rather than peg it at a fixed rate against the dollar. Government economists believed that the ratio of the peso to the dollar would stabilize some-where between 15 and 20 percent of its previous rate. Instead, international investors holding Mexican pesos or debt quickly began selling off their pesos, leading to a significant decline in its value. Wall Street firms in New York had, prior to 1994, purchased large amounts of Mexican debt that were known as *cetes* because of their significantly higher returns. The unstable political situation in Mexico after January, 1994, led most of these firms to pressure the Mexican government to issue devaluation proof bonds known as *tesebonos*. Many of these bonds were short-term issues, and $10 billion of them came due in the first two months of Zedillo's administration. Zedillo's government did not have adequate reserves to pay off all of these obligations in such a short period, and investors began rapidly selling off these bonds. Mexico requested assistance and received a loan from the U.S. Treasury and the International Monetary Fund. Ultimately it was able to meet its obligations, and it paid back the loan early.

In spite of meeting its obligations, the credit crisis produced a general economic crisis as capital fled the country, inflation increased significantly, and economic growth declined, leading to high levels of unemployment. Numerous companies went out of business, and interest rates charged by private banks increased dramatically. It took Zedillo's government two years under an austerity program to return Mexico to a high rate of economic growth. Nevertheless, many Mexicans suffered from the downturn in the economy.

PART III

MEXICO'S PRESENT AND FUTURE

10

MEXICO'S DEMOCRATIC CONSOLIDATION

POLITICS OF DEMOCRACY

Why was the 2000 presidential race essential to Mexico's democratization?

Democratic theorists argue that one of the ultimate political tests of a democratic political model is that national elections are characterized by an alternation in power, especially in the executive branch, where most of the decision-making authority has resided in Mexico. Mexico's 1994 presidential election can be considered competitive and significantly fair, but the incumbent party continued in office, completing more than seventy years in power. In 2000, the National Action Party (PAN) ran the former governor of Guanajuato, Vicente Fox, as its candidate. Fox represented an entirely new type of candidate for the presidency. He was the first PAN candidate to combine a successful political career at the national and state level, with a highly successful business career—as, in Fox's case, the CEO of Coca-Cola of Mexico. Fox was a charismatic campaigner and broadened the appeal of the PAN well beyond its typical partisan supporters. The Institutional Revolutionary Party (PRI) ran Zedillo's former government secretary, Francisco Labastida, a career politician in the federal bureaucracy who had also served as governor of his home state of Sinaloa. Once again the PRD nominated Cárdenas.

Early in the race it became apparent that the presidential contest was between Fox and Labastida. As Election Day approached, polls indicated the two candidates were neck and neck, too close to call the outcome. But in the week preceding the election, when no more public polls were permitted, private polls revealed a significant shift among independent voters, favoring Fox. Scholarly polls and exit polls revealed that while Labastida outscored Fox on all other criteria, Fox exceeded Labastida significantly on one criterion: that of change. Mexico's 2000 election is a benchmark election not only because an opposition candidate won the presidency for the first time since 1929, but also because voters believed that a change in leadership as well as a change in the political model was necessary. Fox generated high expectations about how change and a democratic government could improve the lives of all Mexicans. Younger Mexicans, in particular, were drawn to his message of change, the underlying basis of his campaign. The 2000 election results set in motion other underlying reforms that reinforced democratic governance, while at the same time created expectations the Fox administration could not fulfill, leaving some Mexicans dissatisfied with democratic governance.

Who is Vicente Fox?

Vicente Fox is a unique figure in Mexican politics. He grew up in Guanajuato, a state in west-central Mexico, within a successful farming family. He spent a year as a high school student in the United States, where he perfected his English. After attending Jesuit-run schools in Mexico, including his undergraduate education at the Ibero-American University (the first president since 1929 to graduate from a religiously affiliated college), he became a salesman for Coca-Cola of Mexico. He gradually rose through the ranks of Coca-Cola, and eventually became the chief executive officer. He became the first president to have held a significant corporate position and the first to have worked for an internationally affiliated firm. Fox became seriously interested in politics during the 1988 election, when he became a congressional candidate and supporter of the National Action Party (PAN) presidential nominee, Manuel Clouthier, who shared many of Fox's personal and career credentials. Fox, who considers himself to have been a disciple of Clouthier, won his congressional seat.

Developing a taste for politics, he ran on the PAN ticket for governor of his home state in 1989. After an election characterized by fraud and public protests, President Salinas intervened, designating a PAN politician as governor. Six years later, Fox ran again, winning the election. He used his years as governor to demonstrate his political skills and to achieve support among PAN partisans and political leaders as a potential presidential nominee for the 2000 election. Considered an outsider because he had little experience inside the party bureaucracy, Fox created his own organization, the Friends of Fox, to cultivate and attract independent as well as PAN voters to finance his race for the presidency. He won his party's nomination and defeated the PRI in the 2000 presidential election. In retrospect, Fox can be seen as a highly successful campaigner and was much more successful winning office than governing. He appealed directly to his popular constituency rather than mastering the intricacies of governing, leaving office with many of his major proposals unfulfilled.

What was the Transparency Law?

When Vicente Fox became president of Mexico, on December 1, 2000, many Mexicans had expectations that a democratically elected government would be more accountable and transparent. Indeed, the definition of democracy incorporates the concept of transparency, which makes the government more accountable to the people. A number of interested nongovernmental organizations worked with the executive branch to craft a new law that would require all federal executive branch agencies to provide information on request, as long as it met certain requirements and fell within the purview of the agency. For example, personnel files or information that would compromise national security would not be accessible. It could be considered similar to the Freedom of Information Act in the United States. On June 3, 2002, the Transparency of Access to Public Government Information law was enacted, and one year later it was implemented. Its passage was considered a milestone by many groups. It established an independent agency, the Federal Institute for Access to Public Information (IFAI), to implement the program.

One of the limitations of the legislation is that federal institutions are only required to provide information that is already available in an existing document, rather than to create a document with new information. Nevertheless, many agencies have created new documents to provide requested information. Critics allege that some agencies are not forthcoming in providing adequate answers or any information to appropriate questions. Sometimes the answers to the same questions may be different. One of the strengths of Mexico's transparency program is its accessibility. The IFAI encourages individuals to use the Internet to make requests. Requests that are public through this medium are recorded online, and both the request and the answer are available to anyone who wishes to search a specific agency's responses or a specific subject matter. Furthermore, the IFAI requires that the appropriate agency respond to a request in a short period of time (thirty business days), and although an agency may request an extension, it can do so for only several weeks.

What is "Amigos de Fox"?

When Vicente Fox decided to become a candidate for his party's nomination for the presidency, he created an organization to enhance his nomination prospects and to strengthen his prospects for winning the general election. Established in 1999 by a close friend, Amigos de Fox became a critical non-profit organization for raising funds for his campaign and for attracting supporters. Fox was the candidate of the Alliance for Change, which included the National Action Party (PAN) and Mexico's Green Party. He was also supported by the candidate of the defunct Authentic Party of the Mexican Revolution (PARM). Traditionally, prior to 2000, the PAN had a small partisan base among likely voters in Mexico. Most surveys during that period indicated that 20 to 25 percent of the voters could be considered core partisan supporters of the PAN. Consequently, no presidential candidate from the PAN could hope to win the election without strong support from independent voters, as well as voters defecting from some of the other major parties. Analysts believe the Amigos de Fox organization was essential to the electoral victory of Fox, who defeated the candidate of the Institutional Revolutionary Party by winning 43 percent of the national vote. Some observers believe that as many as four million individuals joined the Amigos de Fox organization. After the election, the leaders of the organization were accused of accepting illegal contributions from abroad and from Mexico. The PAN was eventually fined $50 million for these violations.

What was the role of the private sector in the democratic consolidation?

During the 1980s and 1990s, when the democratic transition reached its apex, the Mexican private sector began a shift in attitude toward partisan politics. In the preceding decades, the private sector rarely became involved in opposition electoral politics. Most businessmen who were involved typically provided free or discounted logistical support for Institutional Revolutionary Party (PRI) campaigns. Larger businesses pursued a neutral policy during elections because they were afraid of reprisals from the government if they openly supported candidates opposed to PRI. Some of the private sector interest group organizations began urging their members to take a more proactive and assertive role in supporting their personal choices for public office. The most influential business organization that encouraged their members to pursue such a strategy was the Mexican Association of Businessmen (Coparmex), the independent business organization in Mexico with the largest membership. Similar business organizations were part of the government-controlled corporatist system that required businesses with a certain number of employees to belong to government-created organizations. Coparmex had been founded in Monterrey, the most important industrial center outside of Mexico City, and the site of numerous global, capital-intensive industries.

Coparmex leadership pursued two complementary strategies in the late 1980s. It persuaded businessmen in their local communities to run for public office, first as mayors, then as governors. These individuals typically were active leaders of the local Coparmex branches as well as other business organizations such as the Chamber of Commerce. As these non-professional politicians increasingly succeeded as candidates of the National Action Party, their presence introduced changes within the party as well as changes in the electoral arena. PRI itself began identifying and nominating respected business leaders to run for public office. The success of these individuals led to other business leaders providing financial support for local campaigns, an essential element in leveling the electoral playing field against the PRI. The efforts of the business community helped bring about electoral competition sooner than otherwise would have been the case.

What are the most important interest groups?

Similar to many countries with electoral democracy and a capitalist economic system, certain actors are predominant in influencing or attempting to influence public policy. In Mexico, the most influential institutional groups are the leading business organizations, some of the labor unions, and, indirectly, the Catholic Church. The group that exercises the greatest influence on public policy, specifically in the economic arena, is the Mexican Council of Businessmen, an elite self-governing organization of approximately forty of Mexico's leading capitalist families. This small group of individuals meets regularly with members of the economic cabinet and occasionally with presidents. They exercise a significant influence on government policy because their combined business interests account for the majority of the major publicly held companies in Mexico. Most Mexicans have never even heard of this organization, which has been expressing its views collectively and individually since it was founded in the 1960s. One of the most serious criticisms of Mexico's economy is the continued presence of monopolistic control in numerous economic sectors, such as telecommunications and television, and the unwillingness or inability of the Mexican government to reduce or eliminate such noncompetitive conditions.

In the past, Mexican unions were important to sustaining the vote-getting ability of the Institutional Revolutionary Party (PRI). But as the democratic transition began taking hold, some unions increasingly became independent of the party and the government. The most important union today, and the most populous, is the National Teachers Union (SNTE), led by Esther Elba Gordillo. The SNTE has effectively used the union's clout to create its own political party, forming political alliances with the National Action Party (PAN) to obtain representation in the Chamber of Deputies. It became a crucial, decisive contributor to Felipe Calderón's electoral victory in 2006. The union is also so powerful that it has prevented necessary reforms to the educational system, especially reforms in the hiring of teachers.

Finally, there exist other actors who tend to exercise an indirect rather than a direct influence. The most important independent institution is the Catholic Church, which has and can play an important political role, such as reinforcing the democratic transition and electoral process, and taking strong positions on social and moral issues, such as abortion. This does not mean that it has been able to prevent legislation at the local or state level that is contrary to its moral positions, such as on abortion, but the executive branch is cognizant of its potential influence over the laity in many areas. The Church also has directly influenced significant political issues, including taking an assertive public position against Vicente Fox's administration when it attempted to bring a legal suit against Manuel Andrés López Obrador as a means of preventing him from running for president in 2006.

What was the role of the media in the process of democratic consolidation?

The Mexican media has become a critical voice in Mexico's democratic consolidation. The media increasingly professionalized its functions and goals, including the view that it should help educate Mexican citizens about their responsibilities as voters and participants in the democratic process, as well as use investigative reporting to ensure greater transparency and accountability among public institutions. The media has successfully carried out that mission, notably using survey research to convey public opinions on various policy issues and to determine voter preferences during and immediately before local, state, and national elections. Such polls were crucial to legitimizing and making possible Vicente Fox's victory in the 2000 election, and to reinforcing the legitimacy of the Federal Electoral Court and the Federal Electoral Institute in its decisions concerning the narrow victory of Felipe Calderón in the 2006 election.

While the media continues to pursue an active role in investigating public malfeasance and other noteworthy subjects of interest to the public, it has become a victim of the power and influence exercised by Mexican drug cartels. The cartels have murdered dozens of journalists who have pursued stories about the cartels and their connections to political leaders. They have threatened publishers and reporters as well as their families. These threats, combined with numerous assassinations and kidnappings, have made it impossible for journalists to pursue investigative research into drug-related corruption. Such articles that are published rarely have bylines. This situation, which the government is powerless to combat, significantly decreases the ability of the media to help enforce greater transparency and accountability, weakening Mexico's ability to achieve a more complete democratic consolidation.

What role did intellectuals play in Mexico's democratization?

Throughout various political periods in the twentieth century, intellectuals have played a significant role in Mexico's political development. Many intellectuals were precursors of the 1910 Revolution, and others joined active revolutionaries in support of their various social and economic positions. In the 1920s, one of Mexico's most prominent intellectual figures, José Vasconcelos, who served as education secretary in the first post-revolutionary government, abandoned the government elites to become the first major opposition presidential candidate against the first formal candidate of the National Revolutionary Party (forerunner of the PRI) in 1929. A number of intellectuals supported his campaign. In 1939, another leading intellectual figure, Manuel Gómez Morín, like Vasconcelos, a former collaborator of the post revolutionary governments, co-founded the National Action Party, the party which ultimately defeated the PRI for the presidency in 2000. But over the years, most intellectuals sought public employment either through government agencies and the foreign service or through major public universities.

Various intellectuals joined or were co-founders of smaller, short-lived political parties, particularly leftist parties, but as a group, they did not exercise a significant impact on the democratization process until the 1980s. Their first notable public act in support of democracy took place in 1986, when many of Mexico's leading figures in the intellectual community signed a full-page announcement in the *Washington Post*, denouncing widespread electoral fraud in the state of Chihuahua. A number of these prominent individuals were affiliated with two leading intellectual publications, *Nexos* and *Vuelta*, and published numerous essays and editorial pieces in these and other leading Mexican newspapers and magazines supporting a democratic transition.

As the 2000 presidential race approached, a large group of influential intellectuals joined with other leading prodemocratic Mexicans from all sectors to form the San Angel Group, which encouraged opposition candidates to participate in the election, including Vicente Fox. Some of these intellectuals, including Jorge Castañeda and Adolfo Aguilar Zinser, following their own personal political ambitions, joined Fox's cabinet as the secretary of foreign relations and national security adviser respectively.

FURTHER CONSOLIDATION

What happened in the 2006 presidential race and how did it strengthen Mexican political institutions?

As the 2006 presidential election approached, each of the three leading parties nominated their presidential candidates. The leading candidate at the beginning of the race was the Party of the Democratic Revolution's former president, Andrés Manuel López Obrador, who resigned his position as governor of the Federal District. He was the most widely recognized of all the candidates, and had developed a loyal following in the capital and the state of México. The National Action Party, the incumbent party, nominated a dark horse candidate, Felipe Calderón, after an intensive primary election. Calderón also had served as his party's president and in Fox's cabinet. Finally, the Institutional Revolutionary Party (PRI), which hoped to make a comeback after losing the presidency in 2000, nominated Roberto Madrazo, the former governor of Tabasco and president of the PRI. As the campaign deepened, Madrazo began to lose ground, and it became apparent toward the end of the race that the contest would be between the PAN and PRD candidates.

When the votes were counted, they revealed that Calderón had come from behind López Obrador, winning the election with only a bare .6 percent of the vote, the closest presidential election since 1929. Equally important, Calderón won only 36.38 percent of the vote, the smallest plurality of any presidential winner since 1910.

López Obrador immediately claimed fraud. He made a formal appeal to the Federal Electoral Court, the only institution with the legal responsibility for adjudicating disputed electoral results, and they examined about 10 percent of the ballots. After extensive research, and issuing a lengthy report, they found no evidence of fraud, but did identify and nullify a number of ballots for both candidates, which did not alter the outcome. López Obrador refused to accept the court's judgment, declaring himself president and encouraging his partisan supporters to boycott the government. Within a few months, despite his intensive efforts to delegitimize the government and the election itself, all but a small minority of core partisans indicated agreement with the court's decisions and viewed both the court and the Federal Electoral Institute that conducted the election as legitimate institutions. These results, despite the intense controversy, suggest support for the culture of law and for democratic institutions, which contributes to the consolidation of Mexico's democracy.

Why did Felipe Calderón win the election?

Most analysts would not have predicted the victory of Felipe Calderón in the presidential election of 2006 just a year prior to the event. Indeed, when he received the nomination of the incumbent National Action Party, he was the least well-recognized of the three leading party presidential nominees. Moreover, many voters, including independents, who had supported his predecessor, Vicente Fox, were disappointed with Fox's inability to produce significant changes as Mexico's first opposition party president. Therefore, Calderón had to overcome the doubts of some of those voters in order to succeed. On the other hand, Fox remained personally popular among Mexican citizens, which helped to neutralize some of his administration's failures. As leading observers noted, the 2006 election was the PRD's candidate Manuel Andrés López Obrador's race to lose. To catch up and defeat AMLO, as he was popularly referred to in the press and by the public, Calderón had to run an aggressive campaign. Initially, he presented himself as a social conservative. About halfway through the campaign, he made a conscious decision to present himself as a centrist and to reinforce those accomplishments, especially economic, that could be attributed to Fox's administration.

As the campaign became more intense, Calderón and his advisers decided to present López Obrador as a radical. They even likened him to President Hugo Chávez of Venezuela, who had alienated many Mexicans after criticizing President Fox. Other groups, including private sector leaders, reinforced this image through their own communications, including on the Internet. If one examines carefully the composition of the Calderón voter, several significant characteristics emerge. His typical voter was female, young—especially younger than 49—was from an upper-income category, was college-educated, was a resident of the northern and central states (long PAN strongholds), was a resident of larger communities, was a Fox voter in the 2000 election, was a resident of states led by PRI and PAN governors, and was positive about Mexico's future economic situation. Calderón also was a stronger performer among those voters who identified themselves in the ideological center. Significantly, although López Obrador's strongest campaign emphasis was on social programs directed toward alleviating Mexico's widespread poverty, Calderón received a large percentage of his support from Mexicans living in poverty but who were beneficiaries of the antipoverty programs begun by presidents Zedillo and Fox.

Who is Manuel Andrés López Obrador?

Manuel Andrés López Obrador is one of the most influential and unique political figures in Mexico in the last decade. Born and raised in the Gulf state of Tabasco, he grew up in a modest family. At an early age he became interested in politics and became a disciple of a socially conscious Institutional Revolutionary Party (PRI) politician from his home state. After first pursuing a career in the government party and ultimately being blocked from advancing within that party, he joined the Democratic Current within the PRI and then the Party of the Democratic Revolution (PRD), and ran as a candidate for governor of his home state against Roberto Madrazo, a leader of the traditionalist, antidemocratic wing of the PRI in a fraud-filled election in 1994. In 1999, he took over the presidency of the PRD, and when elections were held for only the second time for governor of the Federal District, López Obrador won in 2000. As governor of the Federal District, López Obrador was able to demonstrate his administrative skills and his social and economic policy preferences. He introduced a number of innovative programs, including antipoverty programs designed to improve the economic status of Mexico's elderly population. He could be described as a populist with a charismatic appeal to many

Mexicans. His constant exposure in the national media, which emanates from Mexico City, placed him in an excellent position to capture his own party's nomination, essentially without a formal election. Before López Obrador ran officially as a candidate, the attorney general of Mexico indicated he was going to bring a legal suit against him for violating a legal regulation he ignored as governor. Most observers viewed this decision as an attempt by the Fox administration to derail his presidential ambitions, since if convicted he would be ineligible to be a candidate. He received the backing of many Mexicans, including the Catholic Church, which openly stated that the public wished to consider him as a viable candidate and the government should drop its case. This controversy only gave him more notoriety, and the government withdrew its intention to prosecute López Obrador. Early polls showed that López Obrador was the most widely recognized presidential candidate in Mexico and the most popular among the three leading parties. He failed to win the 2006 election, but his posture determined the characteristics of the election. His refusal to recognize the results of the election as legal, and his continued antagonistic behavior, led to his declining popularity, even among many of his original supporters.

What is the Federal Electoral Institute?

The Federal Electoral Institute (IFE) is an independent agency established by federal law to oversee voter registration and all aspects of national elections. It was initially implemented in 1990 as part of a series of historic electoral reforms, but was incorporated in the Secretariat of Government, a politicized cabinet agency in the executive branch. In 1996, as part of a much broader and deeper reform to electoral laws, the IFE became a completely autonomous agency whose members are selected by Congress. It consists of a president and eight councilors. The regular members are elected for a term of nine years and may not be reappointed. The president is selected for a six-year term and may be reappointed. The establishment of the IFE was a significant step in convincing voters that the 1997 congressional elections and the 2000 presidential elections would be honest and transparent. Each state in Mexico has a local version of the IFE that is responsible for all state and local elections. If disputes occur over electoral results, candidates and parties can formally appeal to the Federal Electoral Court, which is the independent agency responsible for ruling on electoral disputes.

Since their establishment the most important electoral dispute was that of the 2006 presidential election. The candidate of the Party of the Democratic Revolution, Andrés Manuel López Obrador, disputed the honesty of the balloting that favored his opponent, Felipe Calderón, the National Action Party candidate who was declared the winner with a margin of only .6 percent of the vote. Before the election took place, the Federal Electoral Institute received the highest level of public confidence of any government-sponsored agency, on par with the positive attitude Mexicans express toward religious and educational institutions. In spite of the fact that nearly 30 percent of the voters initially believed there had been fraud in 2006, confidence in the IFE and the Federal Electoral Court declined only slightly. Within six months of the election, these two institutions regained their pre-election levels of confidence among ordinary citizens. The level of confidence in these two institutions contributed to the legitimacy of the decisions taken during the 2006 election, and contributed positively to institutionalizing democracy and democratic practices in Mexico.

What do the Mexican people think about the government's war on drugs?

When President Fox increased the government's efforts to destroy the drug cartels operating in Mexico, the public was strongly in favor of his efforts. He decided to significantly increase the Mexican armed forces' role, given the inadequacies of local, state, and federal police in carrying out this specific task. The armed forces in Mexico have consistently been viewed by the Mexican public with a high degree of confidence; thus using them to carry out this mission only enhanced the likelihood that the government's strategy would be viewed in a more positive light. By contrast, the police attract little support or confidence from Mexicans. Fox's government had some successes in its campaign against the major cartels, but when Felipe Calderón came into office, he decided to pursue them much more aggressively than any of his predecessors, arguing that the cartels were increasingly becoming a major threat to Mexican governmental sovereignty, national security, and general well-being. Since 2007, drug-related violence and murders have increased dramatically. This is the result of two complementary forces. First, the government's strategy successfully resulted in the arrests of a number of top cartel leaders, creating a vacuum in leadership. Second, the drug cartels' violence is largely directed against each other in an attempt to wrest control of certain regions from competitors. Because the armed forces and the government federal police have taken much more aggressive actions against drug traffickers, cartels have killed many more representatives of the military, the police, and the public prosecutor's office, and their families than previously.

Despite the fact that 80 percent of drug-related murders have been concentrated in only 6 percent of the counties (municipalities) in Mexico, the actual levels and perceived levels of criminal violence have produced a significant shift in public support for the government's strategy. By 2010, more citizens believed the government would not be able to defeat the cartels than believed they could succeed. By the fall of 2010, important institutions and the public increasingly expressed the view in polls or to the media that the government should consider other strategies to cope with drug traffickers, including negotiating with the cartels. Former presidents Zedillo and Fox have both called for the legalization of some drugs, believing that the interdiction strategy is not working in Mexico. The Catholic Church also has begun to express doubts about the wisdom of Mexico's war on drugs, as human rights violations by the military and security forces have increased significantly and the violence continues unabated.

What impact does the army's mission against drug cartels have on civil-military relations?

Beginning in the early 1980s, under President Miguel de la Madrid, the government requested that the army take on an active role in reducing the influence of drug traffickers in Mexico. During his administration and that of his successor, the armed forces largely confined their efforts to eradicating the production of drugs rather than interdicting drug dealers. By the time of the Zedillo administration (1994–2000), the executive branch believed it was necessary to ask the military to pursue a more direct strategy against the traffickers themselves in cooperation with U.S. agencies, including the Drug Enforcement Agency and the attorney general. In return for taking a more active role in the pursuit of drug traffickers, the armed forces requested and received a more active voice in determining national security policy and receiving improved intelligence cooperation from Mexican civil agencies involved in combating the cartels, especially from Public Security and from the attorney general. President Calderón increased the armed forces' role even more dramatically after 2007, expanding to more than fifty thousand the number of troops and officers assigned to this task, and sending mobile units to drug-related hot spots throughout the republic.

The decision to increase the military's role has been made by civilian authorities, including the president, but some analysts fear that in performing what typically are considered

civilian police functions, the armed forces are further delegiti-
mizing the police specifically and civilian institutions generally in the eyes of the Mexican public. Numerous active-duty
officers and retired officers have taken posts in security positions at the state and local levels. On the local level, friction
between the army and civilian police has been reported by the
media, usually the result of corrupt local police officials.
Government officials argue that they have no choice but to
assign the military to performing this task until an adequate
civilian police force at the state and national level can be
created. Efforts are under way to implement such professionalization and vetting processes, but to date these programs
have not been successful in eliminating corruption or in
replacing the military in carrying out these tasks.

How do Mexicans define democracy and how committed are they to democratic governance?

In the last ten years, new survey research by academics and
the media has made it possible to better understand how
Mexican citizens conceptualize democracy and what this
might mean for Mexico's ability to achieve a consolidated,
liberal democracy. Initial research from two surveys that were
supported by the Hewlett Foundation suggests several
important characteristics about the way in which Mexicans
view democracy compared with other societies. Perhaps the
most important overriding feature of citizens' views of
democracy in Mexico is that Mexicans do not express any
consensus as to what it means. For example, does democracy
mean liberty or social equality or progress? It is easy to
imagine that the less consensus that exists about its meaning,
regardless of what that might be, the more difficult it would
be to implement a democratic consolidation and agree on its
procedural rules. The second important aspect of how
Mexicans view democracy is that approximately half of all
Mexicans were equally split between two important views of

democracy, liberty and freedom on one hand and equality on the other. Other Mexicans viewed it as voting and elections, type of government, lawfulness, and progress. To compare Mexican views with the United States, nearly two-thirds of Americans viewed democracy as liberty, followed by only 8 percent who defined it as equality.

Mexican support for democracy is also affected by the way in which they conceptualize it. In the first two highly competitive elections where a party other than the Institutional Revolutionary Party won the election, 2000 and 2006, those Mexicans most likely to view their country as a democracy were those citizens whose candidate won the election. The view that one lives in a democracy only if one's candidate wins an election produces tenuous support for a democratic model. Surveys also discovered, fortunately, that after a relatively short period of time, the percentage of Mexicans who viewed their country as a democracy eventually returned to pre-election levels. Finally, more recent surveys from the comprehensive Latin American Public Opinion project, which compares Mexico with other Latin American countries, also suggests that a sizeable minority of Mexicans, who view democracy as progress or equality, would be willing to return to an authoritarian model if their definition of a democratic political model does not fulfill their expectations.

What do Mexicans expect from democracy?

When Mexicans began a period of democratic transition in the 1980s, the focus among political leaders, ordinary Mexicans, and scholarly observers was on elections and how fair and free they might be. Elections are the most common and basic process through which democracy is achieved. Having free and fair elections also is a defining component of what many citizens, including Mexicans, believe democracy to be.

When Mexicans are asked what they expect from democracy, most citizens expect such a political model to produce economic and social benefits that would improve their standard of living and their quality of life. This expectation would be the same for other political models. Such outcomes are more important to most Mexicans than the degree of liberty and freedom democracy might provide, in contrast to the semi-authoritarian model that existed from 1929 to 2000. How Mexicans define their expectations of democracy affects their evaluation of governmental and presidential performance. For more than a decade, most Mexicans have viewed the country's most serious problems as economic. Indeed, if all the economic issues are combined, more than half of Mexicans consider economic growth, inflation, and poverty to be the number one issue, followed by personal security. In the 2006 presidential election, the two leading candidates, Felipe Calderón from the National Action Party (PAN) and Andrés Manuel López Obrador from the Party of the Democratic Revolution, were within .6 percent of each other when the votes were tallied. In spite of the fact that López Obrador heavily stressed the alleviation of poverty as his primary campaign issue, Calderón won the election. Many analysts believe Calderón won the election because a sizeable percentage of voters who came from modest economic circumstances and were the beneficiaries of government anti-poverty programs in place under the Vicente Fox administration, especially the Oportunidades program, voted for Calderón. Thus Calderón, as a representative of the incumbent party (PAN), benefited from the expectation that his new democratic government would improve the quality of their lives.

11

CULTURAL, ECONOMIC, AND
SOCIAL DEVELOPMENTS

What are Mexican religious beliefs and religious relationships?

The World Values Survey, which is the most comprehensive global survey of citizen values and attitudes, clearly demonstrates that Mexicans view themselves as strong believers in God. Indeed, 98 percent said they believed in God compared to 96 percent of Americans. Nine out of ten Mexicans also believe that God is important in their life and that they receive comfort and strength from religion. Regardless of their beliefs and whether or not they attend religious services, three-quarters of Mexicans described themselves as religious. This description might surprise some readers given the fact that much of Mexican political history in the nineteenth and twentieth centuries involved conflicts between church and state, and the suppression of the Church by the Mexican government. Nevertheless, with the exception of the state of Tabasco, where local suppression of the Catholic Church and all other religions was extreme in the 1920s and 1930s, Christian beliefs are widespread throughout the country. Approximately 85 to 89 percent of the population is self-described as Catholic, followed by Protestants at 5 to 8 percent, most of whom fall into the evangelical category. A tiny percentage claims no formal beliefs or is atheist. Nearly half of all Catholics report attending church regularly, a figure typically much higher than found elsewhere in Latin America, and three-quarters attend religious services once or more a month. Most Mexicans believe it is important to celebrate births and marriage through a religious service.

Religion, and particularly the Catholic Church, has become more influential in the last two decades, in part because of the removal of a number of religious restrictions in the Constitution in 1992. The Catholic Church views itself as providing leadership in spiritual matters, but it is willing to take public positions on other, secular issues, including human rights, democracy, economic welfare of the population, and such moral issues as drug addiction and abortion. For example, Church leaders have been critical of the negative economic consequences of the North American Free Trade Agreement on poorer Mexicans. Recently, they also have raised concerns about human rights abuses by the armed forces in carrying out the government's antidrug strategy. About a fifth of all Mexicans expect the clergy to take public positions on important public policy issues. Consequently, the clergy exercises the potential to influence public opinion. Recently half of all Mexicans say they would listen to the opinions of religious leaders when discussing politics even though two-thirds of citizens believe that such leaders should not influence government. Moreover, half of all Mexicans believe that politicians who do not believe in God are unfit for holding public office. Mexicans over-whelmingly believe their religious institutions provide them with answers to moral problems and spiritual needs.

How is the drug war influencing cultural and religious behavior?

The increased violence in Mexico as a consequence of the internecine battles among drug cartels as well as against the Mexican police and armed forces, and the horrific ways in which attacks have been perpetrated on many Mexicans, has produced some unusual cultural consequences in music and religion. Mexico has a long tradition of generating ballads or *corridos* that interpret numerous aspects of social, economic, and political change. Students of music believe that corridos helped promote popular support for the Mexican Revolution. Thus, it is not surprising, given the presence of drug-related violence and especially the impact of drug trafficking in rural Mexico, that musical groups would take up drug traffickers as a significant topic in their recently labeled *narco corridos.* Regardless of whether the songs present favorable or unfavorable impressions of the various drug traffickers, some of the leading musical performers have become victims of kidnappings and murder. It has never been clarified in the media whether or not these threats and assassinations are reprisals against the singers who support one cartel versus another in their songs, or if some of these individuals are linked to drug traffickers or their families. Mexican officials have been attempting to restrict or ban the performance of narco corridos on the air since 1998 because many songs are seen to glorify the traffickers. The government has put in place some restrictions on their performance on the radio, in nightclubs, and on public transportation. In November 2009, the police chief of Tijuana banned Los Tucanes, a popular group performing narco corridos, after the lead singer addressed two cartel leaders attending an earlier performance and yelled "Mob rules" during the concert.

The other cultural consequence that has received more attention in the United States and in Mexico is the impact that a life of crime and the unpredictability of one's life in confronting numerous other economic setbacks bears on religious beliefs. The most important of such conditions is the increasing emphasis among drug traffickers and other Mexicans on nontraditional religious saints, such as La Santa Muerte (the Saint of Holy Death). They often look like skeletons draped inside of a black or darkly colored sheet, holding a scythe, a symbol of death. As Alma Guillermoprieto recently reported in several essays, such saints are viewed as authentic by many Mexicans, and newsstands even are selling instructional videos that demonstrate how to pray to such saints. The patron saint of desperate causes, St. Jude Thaddeus, also has grown in popularity as numerous cults increase their influence. It is evident, however, that the drug traffickers do not profess or practice traditional moral and spiritual Christianity, but are using perverted or unique religious practices in a desire to protect themselves. Drug traffickers also have increased their impact among some rural communities by donating money to build or refurbish churches even though the Catholic Church specifically has prohibited priests from accepting funds from traffickers.

What are Mexican attitudes toward gender roles?

Mexican attitudes toward gender roles began to change significantly since the 1990s. Male attitudes toward sexual equality are more traditional than the views shared among Mexican women. Mexican women have increased their presence significantly in the economically active work force. The greater presence of women who are employed full-time outside of the home and who live in larger metropolitan areas has altered Mexican views toward family size, the importance of marriage, and other social values related to gender. Thus, nine out of ten Mexicans in 2010 believe women should have the right to work outside the home. Nevertheless, biases persist. When asked if men should be given a preference for employment if jobs were scarce, 28 percent said yes compared with half that number in the United States. A recent survey revealed that 96 percent of respondents believed that women should have equal rights with men. Nearly three-quarters of those who responded affirmatively to this question believed that further changes needed to be made to accomplish such a goal. (Data in this paragraph come from various surveys including the World Values Survey and the Latin American Public Opinion Poll Project.)

Mexican attitudes toward marriage and gender roles also have changed. When asked if a marriage would be more satisfying if both husband and wife worked and took care of their home and children rather than just the husband, three-quarters of all Mexicans responded favorably to that view. Interestingly, those percentages compared favorably to the response given by British citizens. Just eight years ago, the American response equaled that of Mexicans today, suggesting just how dramatic these changes have been in less than a decade. On the other hand, two-fifths of Mexicans continue to believe that a woman has to have children to be fulfilled compared with just 15 percent of Americans. One of the gender biases that has stalled changes in gender attitudes globally is that toward educating males versus females. The traditional bias has always favored boys over girls. In Mexico today, 84 percent disagreed with the statement that a university education is more important for boys than for girls. Only 14 percent of respondents agreed with that statement. Surprisingly, the figure for those who disagreed was actually one percentage point higher than was the case among Americans who were surveyed. Finally, there exists disagreement on whether or not men have greater opportunities to obtain better paying jobs than do women. In the United States, for example, an overwhelming majority believes that to be the case. In Mexico, on the other hand, only 43 versus 55 percent believe men are favored in obtaining those opportunities.

How tolerant are Mexicans of minority groups?

One of the important ways in which we can understand a society's treatment of others who are "different" from them is to examine the level of tolerance characterizing its inhabitants. Survey research has made it possible to compare countries across several measures of tolerance. One way to measure the long-term potential for increased tolerance is to evaluate the degree to which adults consider tolerance and respect for other people as an especially important quality that children should learn at home. For example, four out of five citizens of the United States and Spain considered tolerance to fall into that category in 2000. Mexico scored at the 70 percent level, about the world average. The most common question used in global surveys to test adult tolerance is to ask respondents, from a given list of individuals, who they would not like to have as a neighbor. The World Values Survey of 2000 found that worldwide 43 percent of respondents did not want homosexuals as neighbors, 37 percent did not want those who had AIDS, and 16 percent responded similarly about people of a different race. Mexico's responses to these three categories were: 45 percent, 34 percent, and 15 percent respectively. In the United States, those responses were: 23 percent, 17 percent, and 8 percent. In a 2010 survey by the Latin American Public Opinion Poll Project, 38 percent of Mexicans supported same-sex marriages versus 58 percent of Americans. These figures demonstrate the significantly different levels of tolerance that exist in the two countries toward minorities and other social ills associated with minorities. The comparative data also are revealing in other ways. In the United States, gender, age, levels of education, and income have little effect on the individual responses to the race variable. In Mexico, however, low levels of education and income increase the favorable response to the questions dramatically. Age also affects Mexican responses, but an indicator of future treatment toward minorities is the fact that among the 16–29 age group there exists little difference between the Mexican and American responses. Younger Mexicans also express significantly more tolerance toward neighbors who have AIDs or who are homosexuals.

Many forms of intolerance exist in Mexico, just as they do in other societies. Among the most frequently mentioned examples are religious beliefs, sexual preference, and race. In the first government study of discrimination in Mexico in

2005, the secretary of Social Development reported that nine out of ten homosexuals, elderly, people with disabilities, and indigenous minorities considered they were subject to discrimination. One in five indigenous Mexicans claimed they had been rejected for a job on the basis of race. Mexicans of African descent were not even analyzed in the study. Women also were discriminated against, but Mexicans singled out the four previous groups as most subject to discrimination. The most prominent symbol of the violation of the rights of women in Mexico are the unsolved murders of hundreds of women in Ciudad Juárez over more than a decade, a tragedy which has received international as well as national attention. Perhaps the most intense discrimination in Mexico is toward gay people. Some changes have occurred in recent years. The most tolerant setting for gays is in the nation's capital. The local legislature passed a civil unions law in 2006, and then, in 2010, legalized gay marriages. Mexico created a National Council to Prevent Discrimination, the first such federal agency, in 2003.

Religious persecution has also been a serious issue in Mexico. Numerous conflicts occurred between evangelical Protestants and Catholic communities, especially in rural areas, from the 1960s through the 1990s. It has been estimated that by 2000, approximately 30,000 Protestants were displaced or killed in these confrontations. There also exists a linkage between ethnicity and religious affiliation since indigenous Mexicans are twice as likely as all other Mexicans to convert to evangelical faiths, and the geographic distribution of evangelicals is heavily concentrated in states with large indigenous populations. Another combined source of discrimination is that of female indigenous Mexicans, who are much less likely to receive formal education.

What is Mexico's impact on cultural trends in the United States?

Long before Mexican immigrants accounted for a large percentage of the American population, Mexico exerted an influence on U.S. culture. Over a period of many decades, Mexico exerted a significant influence on American art and architecture. The most influential group of painters formed a generation of artists known as the "muralists." The muralists reflected a significant, socioeconomic artistic movement in Mexico during the revolutionary decade of 1910, in which a number of painters viewed public access to painting as a critical function of art. These painters believed that art should be viewed by the public in general, and therefore should be made available in public settings and on public walls and ceilings. Given the many economic, social, and nationalistic themes that emerged from the revolution, painters such as Jose Clemente Orozco and Diego Rivera began painting murals, using the fresco technique, with political and social messages. Their art was supported by the Mexican government in the 1920s, and both also created works in the United States. But perhaps the greatest impact of this movement was the emulation of public support for art, and its use in public buildings, that occurred during the depression, when the Roosevelt administration employed artists to decorate train stations, post offices, and other buildings with art, sometimes using techniques these artists had learned in Mexico. Other painters, who joined their peers in the United States, added their own palette and flavor, including Rufino Tamayo, who for much of his career was better known in New York than in Mexico. The influence of architectural style, especially in housing throughout the southwest, can be found everywhere.

Today, the most widely influential impact of Mexico on popular culture in the United States is through music, cuisine, and language. Breakfast foods, for example, have been revolutionized in America as a result of Mexican influences, ranging from the ever-present burrito to huevos rancheros. Mexican salsas of all flavors and composition are widely used at sports events, movie theaters, and home entertainment. Multiple fast-food chains specialize in Mexican food. Grocery stores stock more items originating from Mexico than any other ethnic cuisine in the world, including beers, beans, hot sauces, peppers, tortillas, and so forth. Corona is the best-selling foreign beer in the United States. Mexican foods such as guacamole and Caesar salad are so commonplace that they have lost their identity as originating from Mexico. The use of Spanish words and Mexican slang is pronounced in everyday American language, ranging from mano a mano to macho, enchilada to margarita, and rancho to hacienda. The musical influence has kept pace with cuisine. In 2010, the *New Yorker* magazine ran an extensive article about Los Tigres del Norte, who represent the norteño musical style and come from San Jose, California. They boast a huge following among music fans.

12

WHAT LIES AHEAD?

It is clear from the answers to the previous questions that Mexico faces numerous difficult challenges in the immediate future. Some of these challenges are long-term, others are more immediate. Regardless of which issue one places at the top of their list, most will be affected directly or indirectly by Mexico's economy and by its economic and geographic linkages to the United States. The most important challenge facing Mexico is therefore its ability to increase its economic growth while simultaneously reducing high levels of poverty. The lack of consistent growth has plagued Mexico for decades, especially since the early 1970s. A comparative analysis among leading Latin American economies with Mexico clearly demonstrates that Mexico has fallen behind such countries as Brazil and Chile, whether measuring yearly economic growth or decreasing rates of poverty. There are numerous reasons why Mexico has not been as successful in its economic achievements, including the lack of competitiveness in numerous economic sectors, the lack of labor flexibility, the low levels of transparency, and the high levels of corruption. Mexican leadership has continued to increase federal funding for social spending, including its successful *Opportunidades* antipoverty program, but when unemployment is increasing because of low rates of economic growth, poverty levels will increase or remain stable. Mexico has demonstrated under presidents Zedillo and Fox that similar to Chile and Brazil, it could reduce poverty levels, but it needs to reinforce the variables that will provide greater consistency in its economic growth rates. This pattern is even more important in the next decade as the country's reliance on petroleum revenues' contribution to federal funding will decline. These internal limitations and obstacles are under Mexico's control, and in spite of achieving a democratic electoral process, and increasing the power of the judicial and legislative branches of government, it has not successfully addressed the fundamental economic issues. The one significant economic variable over which Mexico exerts little influence is its economic relationship with the United States. One of the reasons why Brazil and Chile continued to boast higher economic growth rates is that they are not tied so strongly to the U.S. economy and therefore have not been nearly as adversely affected by the recession.

The second issue that faces Mexico—and that receives far more attention from American policy makers and the media—is its security situation. In spite of increased cooperation between the United States and Mexico, the assistance package through the Mérida Initiative provided by the United States, and the introduction of legal reforms, organized criminal activity and drug-related violence have not declined as President Calderón begins his fifth year in office. In fact, the level of violence has increased. The Mexican public has become increasingly discouraged about their actual and perceived level of personal security. Since 2009, they no longer believe that the federal government can defeat the drug trafficking organizations, even with the armed forces playing a leading role in the government's antidrug strategy. The increasing growth of organized crime and its expanded entrenchment in other illegal activities, which can be aptly described as economic diversification, ranges from kidnapping for ransom and control of overland illegal migration routes to the United States to sales of illegal goods and products outside of drugs and to the implementation of protection rackets that extort payments from small and large businesses alike. Citizen attitudes toward these conditions have been translated into direct political behavior and explain the National Action Party's significant loss to the Institutional Revolutionary Party in the 2009 congressional elections.

More important than its impact on these elections is the ability of the Mexican government to maintain sovereign control over governmental institutions at the local and state levels. Governmental sovereignty, personal security, and reducing the presence and influence of drug trafficking are all linked to Mexico's economic challenges. One of the reasons why drug trafficking organizations can attract new recruits is the level of poverty and the lack of economic opportunity in Mexico, a condition exacerbated by the recession in the United States and the significant decrease in illegal immigration from Mexico to the United States. Our own intelligence agencies estimate that approximately 450,000 Mexicans are employed in the drug trade. The United States, of course, exerts a far greater economic influence over this criminal activity and its growth by being the largest market for illegal drugs in the world, most of which are produced in or shipped from Mexico. These criminal organizations are strongly linked to criminal gangs in the United States and in Canada, and consequently, play a role in our own social problems with crime. Mexico cannot adequately address its economic issues nor its organized crime issues, without an American proactive strategy to reduce drug consumption and increase our attention toward economic assistance related to antipoverty programs in Mexico. Both countries are spending most of their resources on the consequences of crime and poverty, not on the causes.

The third issue Mexico has to confront is the impact these and other conditions are exerting on democratization. Mexico is an electoral democracy; most observers believe it now boasts free and fair elections. On the other hand, Mexico has disappointed many citizens as well as analysts in their expectations of what a democratic polity would bring to the country and to its citizens. For example, one of the essential features of a functioning democracy is accountability and transparency. In 2003, President Fox oversaw the implementation of a new Transparency Law. This law required all federal agencies to provide answers to questions posed by ordinary citizens, journalists, researchers, and others unless they infringe on personal, confidential information and national security. Thousands of requests have been made and answered. But since the implementation of the law, instead of broadening citizen access and answering their questions, numerous agencies have increased their resistance to responding to all legitimate questions. Perhaps even more disturbing is Mexico's lack of progress on human rights abuses under a democracy. The government's antidrug strategy, and its reliance on the armed forces to implement this strategy, has led to a dramatic increase in human rights allegations and abuses. Yet the government's track record since 2000 in investigating the allegations and in bringing charges against the perpetrators, often the armed forces, has been poor at best. The rule of law is one of the essential ingredients that defines a democratic society, yet the implementation of the rule of law in Mexico is seriously flawed in this and other, numerous respects.

The failure to address these and other pressing conditions described above—many of which are incorporated in the universal definition of a consolidated, democratic model, and if practiced would fulfill most of the conditions associated with a democratic society—is not only disappointing to the expectations of millions of Mexicans, but also as is true elsewhere in many parts of Latin America, has led to citizen dissatisfaction with democracy as a political model. In the most recent round of survey research by the Latin American Public Opinion Project in 2010, 15 percent of Mexicans indicated their approval "of people participating in a group working to violently overthrow an elected government." Mexico ranked in the middle of Latin American countries, including Brazil and Argentina, while Uruguay ranked at the bottom and Belize and Honduras ranked at the top in the percentage of respondents favoring such an activity. One of the variables researchers identified that explain a respondent's willingness to support such a radical strategy was their own personal experience with corruption. Mexicans view corruption as a serious problem, and that it is the primary cause of the government's inability to solve drug-related violence.

Mexicans, like most Latin Americans, are seeking a government that can produce concrete results in solving long-standing issues related to economic and social development, as well as to flawed government accountability and integrity. There are no short-term solutions to these issues. It is likely that current dissatisfaction with government policies will be translated into a change of control over the federal executive branch in Mexico in the 2012 presidential elections in favor of the previous, long-time incumbent PRI. But the PRI's track record in the legislative branch since 2000, and in the executive branch prior to 2000, indicates little likelihood that it has the will or political skill to address these same issues more effectively than the incumbent government. Regardless of which party is victorious in 2012, most of the issues facing Mexico in 2000 will still be at the front of the country's political agenda during that election and throughout the next presidential administration.

CHRONOLOGY OF MEXICAN PRESIDENTS, 1964–2012

2006–2012   Felipe Calderón
2000–2006   Vicente Fox
1994–2000   Ernesto Zedillo
1988–1994   Carlos Salinas de Gortari
1982–1988   Miguel de la Madrid
1976–1982   José López Portillo
1970–1976   Luis Echeverría
1964–1970   Gustavo Díaz Ordaz

SELECTED SUGGESTED READINGS IN ENGLISH

Bailey, John, and Roy Godson, eds. *Organized Crime and Democratic Governability: Mexico and the U.S.-Mexican Borderlands.* Pittsburgh: University of Pittsburgh Press, 2000.

Beezley, William H., ed. *Oxford History of Mexico.* New York: Oxford University Press, 2010.

Bruhn, Kathleen. *Taking on Goliath: The Emergence of a New Left Party and the Struggle for Democracy in Mexico.* University Park: Pennsylvania State University Press, 1997.

Camp, Roderic Ai. *Politics in Mexico: The Democratic Consolidation.* New York: Oxford University Press, 2007.

Camp, Roderic Ai, ed. *The Oxford Handbook of Mexican Politics.* New York: Oxford University Press, forthcoming, 2012.

Council on Foreign Relations. *Building a North American Community.* New York: Council on Foreign Relations, 2005.

Domínguez, Jorge I., and Chappell Lawson, eds. *Mexico's Pivotal Democratic Election: Candidates, Voters, and the Presidential Campaign of 2000.* Stanford, CA: Stanford University Press, 2004.

Domínguez, Jorge I., Chappell Lawson, and Alejandro Moreno, eds. *Consolidating Mexico's Democracy: The 2006 Presidential Campaign in Comparative Perspective.* Baltimore: Johns Hopkins University Press, 2009.

Edmonds-Poli, Emily, and David A. Shirk. *Contemporary Mexican Politics.* Lanham, MD: Rowman & Littlefield, 2009.

González, Francisco E. *Dual Transitions from Authoritarian Rule: Institutionalized Regimes in Chile and Mexico, 1970–2000.* Baltimore: Johns Hopkins University Press, 2008.

Hernández Chávez, Alicia. *Mexico: A Brief History.* Berkeley: University of California Press, 2006.

Hughes, Sallie. *Newsrooms in Conflict: Journalism and the Democratization of Mexico.* Pittsburgh: University of Pittsburgh Press, 2006.

Krauze, Enrique. *Biography of Power: A History of Modern Mexico, 1810–1996.* New York: HarperCollins, 1997.

Morris, Stephen D. *Gringolandia: Mexican Identity and Perceptions of the United States.* Lanham, MD: Rowman & Littlefield, 2005.

Peschard-Sverdrup, Armand B., and Sara R. Rioff, eds. *Mexican Governance: From Single-Party Rule to Divided Government.* Washington, DC: Center for Strategic and International Studies, 2005.

Rodríguez O., Jaime E. *The Divine Charter: Constitutionalism and Liberalism in Nineteenth-Century Mexico.* Lanham, MD: Rowman & Littlefield, 2005.

Selee, Andrew, and Jacqueline Peschard, eds. *Mexico's Democratic Challenges: Politics, Government, and Society.* Washington, DC: Woodrow Wilson Center, 2010.

Thacker, Strom. *Big Business, the State, and Free Trade: Constructing Coalitions in Mexico.* Cambridge: Cambridge University Press, 2000.

Weintraub, Sidney. *NAFTA's Impact on North America: The First Decade.* Washington, DC: Center for Strategic and International Studies, 2004.

INDEX